Giulia Galli

When a Parent is Born

Your Journey toward Intentionality

Giulia Galli
When a Parent is Born
Your Journey Toward Intentionality

All Rights Reserved
Copyright © 2025

1st Edition April 2025

Reegal

DEEPENING ROOTS

REEGAL.CO.UK

GIULIAGALLI.SUBSTACK.COM

To Viola and Leonardo,
the lights of my life

PREFACE

The 2020 pandemic was a turning point that threw many parents into their children's world with a constant 24-hour presence.

People who were used to spending about 4 hours a day at home with family suddenly found themselves staying at home around the clock discovering their children's world and the complexity of their lives.

Some reactions to this change were of quiet wonder, as parents began to understand the magical world of children, teenagers and young people. Others, however, were of 'command-control', triggering conflicts in the family that were mostly incomprehensible to the children: who were these strangers who suddenly entered their lives trying to impose a new rhythm and beliefs?

Since then, therefore, the need to support parents has become increasingly evident. Being a parent with good intentions alone was no longer enough. In an era so virtually connected and with the avalanche of information, lifestyle proposals and all kinds of solutions immediately at hand, it has become necessary to be parents who are up to the task of raising children in the third millennium.

Intentional Parenting has therefore become a philosophy of life to be offered to all parents so that it becomes the *magic key* to opening the doors to a truly extraordinary relationship with their children. It is filling a social void that has for too long been focused on analysing, evaluating and sometimes labelling our children for their attitudes that are unknown to us.

It is filling a space that gave parents too many excuses for blaming the 'system' and especially the school for any possible failings of their children.

This, among other things, created conflicts between parents and teachers that were often incomprehensible to the children.

Visiting numerous companies every year and meeting the people who work there, I have seen first-hand how much parents need to choose how to be the best parents they can be in the few hours a week that they have available outside of work.

In this journey I have found in Giulia great sensitivity, preparation and competence in dealing with these important issues with lightness and effectiveness.

I also found in her a great consistency between what she says should be done and what she herself does with her children.

Her continuous search for professional growth through specific and international courses has been fundamental and her way of communicating with parents in the courses is always full of courtesy, firmness and respect for people who are too often left alone.

From their first interactions with Giulia I saw parents immediately take charge of their role and see things differently, putting their children at the centre of their commitment with the certainty that all of us, parents and children, have only one go on this carousel of life and the smartest thing we can do is live every day, every moment, every breath with intention and fun (whatever difficulties we may face).

I'm confident that in these pages the readers, parents and not only them, will find inspiration to give new meaning to their parental mission, improving their relationship with their children to become the one that they always wanted.

Enjoy the read!

Coach Bruno (Giulia's dad)

Being a Parent

Being a parent is the most demanding job in the world: 24 hours a day, 7 days a week, no time off, no holidays, no salary and absolutely no insurance. It is also the most important job, because of all the jobs in the world it is the one that shapes our children, their future, and the future of the whole of humanity.

A colossal undertaking, the scope of which makes history. Literally: because it shapes the story of our children and the world to come.

Whether we want to see it or not, the results of our parenting choices echo through the generations, leaving an indelible mark.

Yet, to become parents, no official preparation is required. No prerequisites. Unless it's an adoption, none of us have to attend interviews. Nobody asks us to study, to get diplomas, degrees or certificates. Or to pass tests. Let alone to keep up to date.

Isn't it strange that we need certificates and continuous training for any job except ours? And, in any case, will it really be enough to do our best?

Amidst all our commitments, deadlines, pressures, and the thousand problems of everyday life, will it be enough to commit ourselves to raising our children to the best of our ability?

Beyond the long-term impact, the way we parent not only shapes our children's future, but also creates our present. It moulds it.

Our choices are what actually make our days enjoyable or not.

The way we parent is what makes life with our children easier, or messes it up to the point of keeping us up at night. It can make us feel good, great, wonderful, or the complete opposite. It can make us count the minutes until pick-up time, looking forward to returning home, but sometimes also giving us a sudden urge to stay out just a little longer....

It's not probability. It's not genetics. It's not their character.

It's us. And, just to be clear from page one, when I say 'it's us' I don't mean that we are doing something wrong and/ or have done something wrong. Nor that we are in any way wrong.

From my point of view, in light of studies and discussions with dozens and dozens of other parents, the fact is that our job is both the most demanding (and tough, impactful, and tiring, etc.) and the most underestimated.

Information isn't lacking.

The way I see it, what we lack most is an awareness of how monumental the task we are undertaking is. We see the downstream effects: the tantrums, the problems, the difficulties with our children. We torment ourselves, wondering what the cause is: are we the ones who are 'wrong'? Or is it them?

And that's why, at a certain point, many of us look for help and guidance.

'Ah, if only there was a manual...'

In fact there is, and not just one, but thousands I'd say: there are already a lot of pages written and terabytes of data in the form of books, podcasts, videos and more or less scientific publications just a click away.

First as a parent, and then as an Intentional Parenting Coach, I immersed myself in many of these sources.

'Intentional Parenting Coach?'

Okay. A step back.

Nice to meet you, I'm Giulia.

I'm an Intentional Parenting Coach. For a few years now, I've been helping other parents choose what kind of parent they want to be. This is what 'Intentional Parenting' means: intentionally choosing what kind of parents we want to be for our children.

Now, going back to the manuals, in my professional career I have read, studied, listened to, explored and analysed the vast amount of literature available, discovering that most of it still promises 'fail-safe' methods, rigid schemes full of things to do, not to do, and never to do. It seems that every author has their own 'unique' and always 'definitive' method for becoming perfect parents: a more or less long list of rights and wrongs, made up of functional and dysfunctional schemes that are valid for everyone, always.

And here's the problem: for me, and for many others, standard solutions have never worked. Simply because they didn't resonate: they're too far removed from me, from my values, from the dynamics of my family.

This is precisely why I have continued to do research and collect my discoveries, first in a series of courses and now in this book.

Who is this book for?

This book is for parents like you and me, and like many others who read my blog, participate in my workshops, as well as all those who have simply started to ask themselves a few questions about their role. For those looking for an easier, more pleasant, more meaningful way.

For those who dream of less shouting, less frustration, and much more harmony, starting today, and forever.

It's for:

> » Mary and her son Jake, who at 14 years of age refuses to open a book.

> » Helen, who is struggling with two small children and feels as if the weight of the world is on her shoulders.

> » Sophie, mother of a little girl, who wonders if she has already made all the mistakes in the world, and if what she does will ever be enough.

Obviously it's also for dads: the Andres, the Lucas, the Paulos, the Arthurs and the Mattheos.

This book is for parents who feel they are stuck in a kind of swamp, who feel frustrated and tired and are looking for a way out. It's for those who dream of a calmer and happier home. It's for those who don't want to be judged by yet another expert. It's for anyone who wonders what kind of human beings they want to raise. Curious parents looking for a sustainable, personalised approach that is deeply rooted in their reality.

It is also for educators, psychologists and professionals who work with children and families.

It can be useful for all of them.

If, on the other hand, I had to think of a type of reader for whom this book is not useful, it would be parents who already have all the answers, and perhaps even those who have no desire to ask themselves questions.

What you won't find here

This is not a manual, nor a list of instructions.

It's not a plug-and-play system.

You won't find magic wands or universal solutions to all your challenges.

And you certainly won't find judgements, criticisms or rigid ideas of right versus wrong.

Why? Because there is no single way to be a parent.

What will you find here?

If I haven't chosen the wrong title, you should already have an idea.

'When a parent is born' is here to help you ask yourself what kind of parent you want to be. To help you understand that:

> » Your choices matter;

> » You can always choose;

> » It's never too late.

In the next 12 *beacons* and in the appendix, you will find true-life stories, questions, reflections, challenges, techniques and strategies to help you become a more conscious parent, on your terms.

'When a Parent Is Born' is centred on Intentional Parenting: what it means, why it's important, and above all how it can help you and your children.

How to read it?

Imagine you are walking through a forest, not knowing where you are going, with a thousand distractions and a lot of noise.
It is night and the forest is dark.
Suddenly a light appears.
Then another, and another.
As you gradually see more, you realise that you can choose which direction to take. You can decide which path you prefer, the one that is best for you to reach your goal: a home where you and your children feel safe, connected and happy. A home where you will have finally chosen what kind of parent you want to be.

'When a parent is born' is structured as a series of *beacons* of light that, one after the other, can illuminate your journey as a parent, making it clearer and clearer. And enjoyable, fun, stimulating, and very cool.

It's no coincidence that there are 12 *beacons*, like the months of the year and the hours of the day, the signs of the zodiac, the main gods of Olympus, the rings that characterise the earthly experience in Buddhist philosophy, each linked to the next by a cause and effect relationship.

Each one starts with a question and a spoiler, and ends with three 'Takeaways'.

1. 'Generations in the Mirror' takes a look at the generation gap and answers the question "Are our children different?'

2. 'Intentional Parenting': what it is, why it's important and how it can radically transform your family life.

3. 'It all starts with us' is about our personal identity, exploring how we model our way of being parents.

4. 'Inside-Out' is about self-awareness, a skill we can learn that helps us to not react on autopilot but to respond intentionally.

5. 'Our compass' is about our values: our most powerful anchor. Even when the going gets tough and the challenges are super hard.

6. 'Through their eyes' is all about maps of the world, because every human being has their own unique way of seeing things, including our children.

7. 'Our Inner Script' starts with a question 'How can I do it if I already know I can't?' and from here it covers emotions and emotional identity, what influences our thoughts and shapes reality.

8. 'The Bridge' talks about how to build trust, answering the question 'How can I get them to listen?'

9. 'The Frequency' helps us find our children's frequency

so we can connect with them and say goodbye to the feeling of talking to a brick wall.

10. 'Beyond Words' is about active listening, also answering the question: 'Why don't they ever tell me anything?'

11. 'Words matter'... Guess what? It's about how words create worlds: choosing them intentionally helps us and our children, starting today and forever.

12. 'Questions?' Here, the question is: 'How to ask questions?' and it helps us choose when and how to ask them.

'Can I skip a chapter or two?'

Yes, you can, although I don't recommend it because each topic is preparatory to the next. As an author and Intentional Parenting coach, and above all as an intentional parent, I invite you to read the chapters in sequence, letting each *beacon* light your way and guide you towards a deeper understanding of yourself and of those you are raising.

As for the appendix, Stages and Situations, you can choose to read them all, or go directly to the phase that involves you and your children.

THE 12 BEACONS

Imagine returning to a home filled with serenity and connection.
How wonderful would it be to have a relationship with your children based on trust, understanding and intentional communication?
How fantastic would it be to experience a relationship in which conflicts disappear before they even arise?
In this journey we start with you, your generation, your identity, your values as a parent. One *beacon* at a time, you will discover that your choices shape the behavior of your children and the relationship you have with them. Finally, you will be able to align your words and actions with the kind of parent you have chosen to be.
You will be surprised how small changes will create profound transformations, allowing your family dynamics to thrive and your children to grow, shaped by your conscious choices and your Intentional Parenting.

The way we raise our children today shapes the adults of tomorrow. We are responsible for this. I believe in it so strongly that my personal mission, the one that guides my choices, from the first to the last, every single day, is:

'Changing the world through my children'.

Do we want a better future?

Let's say that Intentional Parenting gives us the chance to build it, starting with our children: with awareness, first of all, with intentionality, and with fun.

Do we want more harmony and less friction in our home?

We can always choose. Always.

And you have already done so in some way.

If you are reading this book, even if it was a gift, you are not here by chance: if you are on these pages, it is by choice.

Among the choices that are yours to make, there's also the one to make a difference for those you brought into the world, for your family, for humanity and of course for yourself. For the future, starting from the present.

Happy reading!
Giulia

1/ Generations in the Mirror

QUESTION: Are our
children different
from us?

SPOILER: Every child
is different, every
parent is different
and it's always
the first time for
everyone.

5 June 1924. John is at the kitchen table, drinking coffee, when he sees his son Jack get up and ask permission to speak.

'Father, I would like to ask if I could go to my room'.

'Without even finishing lunch?'

Jack replies that he is sorry, but he has a lot of studying to do.

'Isn't it time to stop with these fantasies?' replies John, who would prefer his son to dedicate himself to things a little more useful than books: a job, for example. At the ripe old age of fourteen, it would be about time. *'Kids today'*. Jack closes himself in his room and, before starting to study, wonders why his father doesn't understand him.

Fast forward to 1964. Jack the engineer is flicking through a newspaper in his armchair when he sees the youngest of his three daughters sneaking towards the door.

'Where are you going, young lady?'

'Downtown, to a rally, with the others...'

'A rally? What for?'

'I mean, you know, I'm doing my part...'

'Wouldn't it be better if you studied instead of wasting so much time with such nonsense?' asks the very concerned engineer.

Lizzie snorts.

'I mean, come on, how can you not understand that it's important?'

'First of all, young lady, could you stop all this 'I mean' stuff?'

For Jack, his daughter speaks an alien language. For Lizzie, her father lives in the Middle Ages.

Fast forward + 60.

Lizzie has become a grandmother. In front of her is her granddaughter who has just had an argument with her parents. She wants to go to a human rights demonstration and they won't let her.

'Then I'll be, like, dead! You know?'

'Not really, dear...'

'I hate them, Grandma... I hate them and I never want to see them again'.

DIFFERENT TIMES AND RECURRING FRICTIONS

Years go by, times change, language and fashions evolve, but the questions seem to keep coming back.

> *Why don't my parents understand?*
> *Why do my children speak 'Klingon'?*

Because every generation[1] is different.

And it is different because it grows up in a world shaped by its own time, immersed in a landscape all of its own, and therefore incomprehensible to those who came before it.

In the last 120 years, we've had seven generations, each with their own values, dreams, language, and approach to life. Each one is unique, each one is different from the others.

Becoming aware of the gap between generations helps us understand why we ourselves may not have understood our parents, and why today we may feel distant from our children.

The truth is that the world keeps changing and people change with it. Technology evolves, transforming the way we communicate, work, and think: every new tool changes our way of seeing life, shaping young people who are inevitably different from those who came before them.

---

1   The word 'generation' was defined in 1965 by sociologist Norman Ryder as 'a group of people shaped by the same historical, social, and cultural forces. These shared experiences forge distinct identities, ways of thinking, and priorities, and often create a seemingly unbridgeable gap between parents and children'.

Take progress, for example.

Boomers and Gen X grew up with little technology, learning to value 'traditional' ideals and building careers often defined by a total, almost obsessive dedication to work. Millennials are said to be more interested in the work-life balance; Gen Z is more open to change and more socially aware; Gen Alpha, born already connected, is a step further: today's kids live in a reality shaped by social media, artificial intelligence, debates about inclusion and climate awareness.

Not only do they have tools and resources that we never even dreamed of, but they are also super-informed on topics that were hardly talked about in the nineties.

Our children live in an era that encourages them to express their feelings, to name their emotions, and to question the world around them. And it is this, even more than progress and AI, that makes them different from us, just as we were different from our parents.

Think about how we were raised and how we turned out. Who we are today also depends on the education we received. And since this applies as much to the positive aspects as to the rest, it's easy to be tempted to attribute our possible weaknesses to them.

'If only they had taught me this and that...'
'My mother never paid me a compliment'.
'For my father, only grades mattered...'
'My parents never understood me'.

Could they have done better?
I doubt it.

Some of us may have been more or less fortunate, but the truth is that our parents, with a few exceptions, did the best they could with the resources they had. Resources that are infinitely more limited than ours today, especially in terms of awareness.

When I think about my personal history, I know I have been privileged in many ways. I was born in the 80s to two parents who were already very ahead of their time. My father, a natural-born coach, was born wise, and my mother, an independent woman, raised me and my sisters in an environment rich in relationships, with a strong work ethic. From a young age, I spent my summer months working in the family hotel. The money I earned working at the reception and tidying the rooms allowed me to go on my beloved study holidays in England, where I learnt to speak English, the language that opened the doors to my career. Looking back, I know that my professional successes are also thanks to my parents, who taught me commitment, responsibility, perseverance and consistency.

They did this through both words and examples. Every decision they made was the result of their love for me and their desire to prepare me for life in the best possible way.

Recently, while preparing for one of my workshops, I asked both of them if they had ever thought about what kind of parents they wanted to be. My father replied: 'For sure, I always wanted to be a consistent parent'.

For him, consistency was - and still is - the alignment of thought, words, and actions, one of his core values.

My mother said she didn't have an ideal parent in mind, but that there were examples she didn't want to follow.

'I know I wanted you to be responsible, autonomous, and

as independent as possible'.

For her, an extraordinary entrepreneur, autonomy was fundamental. That's why she always wanted me to work: to be able to take care of myself, without having to depend on anyone.

Okay, of course, it wouldn't have been bad if both of them had also been a little more interested in my emotions, or in sports. Let's face it: for many parents in the nineties, emotions were certainly not a priority. Far from it. Well before that, there were careers to build and businesses to run, and to do so required discipline, dedication, endurance.

The same goes for sport: it was less important then than it is today.

Again, both of them raised my sisters and me in line with what they believed, to the best of their ability. Just as I'm sure my grandparents did with their children. And as every parent today does with theirs: doing their best, balancing between the world and the ways of yesterday and those of today.

THE AFTERMATH OF YESTERDAY

Some time ago, we were in a very crowded restaurant in central London, sitting just a few centimetres away from a family with two children aged about ten and eleven. At a certain point, the father started insulting the eleven-year-old who, after arguing a little with his chopsticks, had started to eat the noodles with his hands directly from the serving dish. The insults were heavy. Enough to make your ears bleed. We were too close to not hear and he was too furious to hold back.

But what struck me most was what he said next: 'You're lucky, you, that I'm kind and modern! If my father had seen me do something like that, he would have smashed my face. No doubt about it!'

The fact that he had been raised by a 'Cerberus' - one capable of smashing his face in - led him to believe that he was a 'kind and modern' parent!

Meanwhile, around them, and around us, the atmosphere had turned frosty. The whole room was frozen. The mother and little brother were silent. The 11-year-old hadn't said a word: he'd taken the outburst on the chin, without a word.

The second event that stuck with me was the reaction of my son Leonardo, once we left the restaurant. Without me asking anything, he said: 'You can tell that child is used to it...'

Since then I've thought back to that scene on several occasions.

Some of us, as I said, have been lucky. Others, like the father mentioned above, less so. And not only because they were raised with models centred on control, punishment and fear, but because once they become parents, they don't realise they are replicating these models. It's a two-sided coin: on one side there is replication, on the other there is distancing. In turn, the replication and distancing can be voluntary or instinctive.

When we know what we didn't like as children and we make sure not to do it to our own children, then the distancing is conscious, voluntary.

'I am not going to shout, I am not going to get angry, I am not going to lose my temper, I am not going to do this or that... like my mother or father did'.

And if we find ourselves shouting, losing our temper or being overprotective, we say to ourselves: 'I'm just like my mother/I've become my father!'

Reflecting on both myself and the other parents I've worked with as an Intentional Parenting Coach, I see that many of us distance ourselves from the way we were raised, especially when we were young, say before the age of forty, and then 'soften' and eventually come to feel gratitude towards our parents.

Instinctively, without realising it, we tend to repeat the positive behavior that most gratified us as children.

The fundamental difference lies in our level of attention: it's easier for us to recognise and therefore remember what is wrong than what is right.

With our children, we immediately see a tantrum, a rude response, a bad grade or a lack of interest. And also with ourselves: missteps, mistakes and negative experiences immediately catch our eye, while we are less aware of the positive things.

This greater attention/attraction to and for negativity doesn't just fall from the sky, and it's not part of us. It's not how we're made. It's not our 'character' and it's not written in stone.

It's just a *habit* that our brain has developed and then gradually reinforced.

HABITS AND CHOICES

Even though growing up in a certain era or in a certain family is relevant, what matters even more is the specific way in which we choose to respond to our experiences, starting from the cradle. In fact, even earlier.

The point is that, as soon as it begins to form, our brain starts to make choices, selecting the responses that seem most effective to us and discarding all the others.

This means that when we are born, our brain already has a wealth of forty weeks of stimuli, choices and favourite responses. It is anything but a 'blank slate': it already has its own identity and even a favourite operating framework.

We leave a warm, cosy, familiar womb where we have lived 100% of our existence, and are thrown into a cold and completely unknown world.

To enable us to survive out there, our brain knows it has to conserve energy. That means it has to find the most efficient strategies, those that require the least effort and give the best results.

Our brain isn't lazy, it's cautious.

From a biological point of view, efficiency means survival because even the slightest waste of time and/or resources can be fatal.

Faced with each new challenge (an event or a situation), the brain decides how to act and observes the result, memorising it and gradually distinguishing what works from what doesn't work.

For example, if when we cry our mum picks us up straight

away, the brain may decide that crying is a good strategy to get picked up. But if crying makes mummy get upset, the brain may also decide to reduce the tears and try other strategies.

Once the brain gets used to a certain preference, it no longer questions it and from then on it repeats it automatically, often for the rest of our lives.

Unless, at a certain point, the brain starts to question its own preferences, leading us to understand that we are always free to choose what to choose, always. Even when we believe the opposite, when we tell ourselves 'That's the way I am', when we feel trapped in a pattern or when we think we can't change. This infamous 'that's the way I am' often makes us repeat behaviors without even realising it.

Take for example the frustration expressed by parents who have 'gotten used to' scolding their children. Even if they don't want to raise their voice, they believe it's the only way to make their children listen to them. This is a perfect example of how, often without realising it, we fall into old patterns, what some call the 'comfort zone'. The point is that it often has nothing to do with comfort in the common sense of the term.

We are not at all 'comfortable', we are just moving in familiar territory, which Virginia Satir[2] rightly calls the *'familiarity zone'*.

---

2   Virginia Satir was a psychologist considered the mother of family therapy who defined herself as a healer and teacher rather than a therapist. She was convinced that each of us always has the ability to choose because we all have the resources to succeed, but often we don't know how to deal with the problems we encounter, and this is because we don't use the resources at our because we don't use the resources available to us. For Virginia Satir, 'Problems are not the problem, the problem is facing them'.

Familiarity zone?

In a nutshell, the *familiarity zone* is that known area in which we repeat the patterns that seem most recognisable to us and therefore less frightening.

This doesn't mean that it's a nice place, or pleasant or even comfortable; it's just an area that we consider safe because it's the result of established habits, such as reacting in the same way every time our child behaves differently than we expected.

In this area we rely on automatic responses that seem predictable to us, even when they're not useful.

So even if it is familiar (because we know it), it often leads to frustration and a string of very annoying little feelings of guilt.

We can think of the *familiarity zone* as an autopilot mode that allows the brain to save energy by avoiding new solutions and repeating patterns that have worked in the past.

In some cases this is useful, but when it comes to parenting choices (such as yelling to get a child's attention), the *familiarity zone* traps us in habits that are not in line with the kind of parent we want to be.

Staying in it can lead to patterns that hinder our parenting goals (and make our lives less enjoyable than they could be). We know that shouting doesn't help much. Okay, maybe if we shout our children will listen to us, but they certainly don't do it willingly and this could sooner or later lead to resistance, or defiance.

Without realising it, we could find ourselves repeating the

same parenting styles we grew up with, even if they were anything but effective.

Breaking free from the *familiarity zone* and changing these patterns is possible and easier than you might think: it just requires awareness and intentional action.

'No one can make us change. Each of us has a door to change that can only be opened from the inside'.
-Virginia Satir

Aside from our specific preferences, as mentioned above, the environment in which we grow up is extremely influential. By environment, I don't just mean the era or the social context, but also the nest in which we arrive as newborns and grow up as children, teenagers and adults.

When I became a parent, I immediately started wondering what kind of person I wanted to be for my children.

While I continued to think about it, I started reading, studying, watching videos and attending courses. In the meantime, I discovered that more and more people were starting to ask themselves the same question.

This observation prompted me to continue my research and to understand that, since each person is unique, there is no single way to be a parent.

Every parent is a parent in their own way, and every way is different.

TAKEAWAYS

1. **Are our children different from us?** They are growing up in a world we could never have imagined, so it's no surprise that they are different; every child is unique, every parent is unique and every family dynamic is unique.

2. **Our parents' model:** replication or distancing? Although how we were raised is important, **what matters most is how we intentionally choose to react.**

3. **What we call our "comfort zone" isn't comfortable, it's just familiar**: getting out of it is easier than you might think. It just requires awareness and intentional action.

2/ INTENTIONAL PARENTING

QUESTION: When is a
parent born?

SPOILER: When we
start choosing what
kind of parent we
want to be.

Gemma is at breaking point. She has a three-year-old daughter who doesn't eat enough and hardly sleeps. Instead, she cries all the time and throws one tantrum after another. As if that weren't enough, Gemma is overwhelmed by unsolicited advice and constant criticism.

'You should do this, and not that!'

'You're picking her up? You're wrong'.

'You let her cry? Oh my goodness!'

She resists and does her best, but risks exhaustion and in fact for a while now she has been wondering if she made the right choice in becoming a mother, if she is good enough, if she is really capable or, even worse, if she hasn't already ruined everything. She feels wrong and is looking for a way to *fix* herself.

Sarah is on the brink: she has two school-age children who constantly argue, shout and are always on the verge of hurting each other. She is not the only parent, but she is the only one who has to take care of everything, without ever receiving so much as a thank you. And now she is not only tired: just like Gemma, she feels wrong, and just like her, she asks me to *fix* her.

Then there's Kate, who is furious because her teenage son has absolutely no interest in studying. He couldn't care less about school, books, let alone grades. The only thing he does is stay glued to social media, 24/7. After 'having tried everything' with 'that idiot of her son' - as she laughingly calls him - she comes to me to 'fix him'.

THREE MOTHERS, THREE SITUATIONS

Gemma and Sarah feel there is something wrong with them and are looking for tools and methods to fix themselves. The third mother, Kate, instead believes that her son is the one who need fixing.

But what if there's nothing to fix at all? What if there's nothing wrong with anyone?

Surprise: there isn't!

There is nothing broken or wrong, neither for Gemma, nor for Sarah, nor even for Kate or her son: it's just a matter of *sparks* that, at a certain point, can lead all three (and you, the reader) to *intentionality*.

The spark of intentionality

Some people bring a child into the world because they want to, perhaps always have wanted to, while others do it because it just happens. And so, in both cases, at a certain point we find ourselves parents.

Yet, a parent is truly born when they intentionally choose what kind of parent they want to be.

Intentional Parenting can begin in different ways. Perhaps it begins by asking ourselves how we want to raise our children: what values, ideals, and beliefs we want to pass on.

Sometimes, the push to become an intentional parent comes from a specific need, perhaps in parallel with some significant change, or to overcome a somewhat difficult moment, or because we have heard about intentionality from someone else (in a podcast, in books, from other parents).

Or, even more simply, one day we decide that we want to live better with our children, that we want more harmony and less chaos.

The truth is that it doesn't matter what the 'spring' is: what really matters is that sooner or later you get there because, as I will repeat dozens of times in this book, being intentional is the most powerful choice we can make as parents.

In my case, I became an intentional parent by nurturing

my children's minds, one conscious choice at a time. My spark was struck years ago while watching Forrest Gump.

One line in particular: «My mother always said, *Stupid is as stupid does*».

This line struck me for two reasons.

Firstly because it shifts the focus from identity to actions, a fundamental principle when we educate our children. And then it made me wonder *'When my daughter has grown up, what will she remember of the things I tell her?'*

That was a moment of realisation, a true Epiphany!

Wait a minute, I thought, *I don't want to leave it to chance. I want to consciously choose the most important things I want to pass on and repeat them often enough to make them stick.*

That's how my journey began, setting in motion a process that was very reflective and incredibly fun. From that moment on, my mission was to understand who my children were and what specific wisdom I wanted to pass on to them.

At the time, Viola was five years old, already a bright and very serious child, who always tried to do her best. I noticed that sometimes she needed encouragement to just have fun. So I gave her the motto 'The most important thing in life is to have fun'.

On the one hand it was a reminder to relax, laugh and enjoy life; but on a deeper level, it was above all a message for her future: in any situation, when you realise that it's no longer fun for you, when you no longer feel at ease, walk away.

Leo, on the other hand, was fascinated by superheroes and already had a rather carefree approach to life. He didn't need help learning how to have fun, he already knew how to do that! Instead, I wanted to help him unlock the power of learning, to show him that knowledge could be his greatest strength. So I gave him this motto: 'Your secret weapon is learning'.

It was my way of showing him that, just like his heroes, he had a superpower that could make him unstoppable: the ability to learn and grow. I wanted him to understand that learning would set him free. Over time, I saw him fully embrace this idea.

These were my first Intentional Parenting acts, even if I didn't realise it at the time. Now, after years of working as an Intentional Parenting Coach, everything has become clearer: my children are not what they are by chance.

Their personalities are important, of course, as is the environment in which they grow up, in our case South East London. But I know that I have been an intentional parent from the start.

I have deliberately chosen the kind of parent I want to be, especially in difficult situations and when faced with the unexpected. I have tried to leave little room for impulsive reactions, instead seeing every moment as an opportunity for growth for both my children and myself.

In practice, being intentional parents doesn't mean being perfect, but having a direction and a purpose. It's about recognising that every choice we make, big or small, shapes the kind of people our children will become. So I keep reminding Viola, through life's challenges and triumphs: 'The important thing is to have fun'. And I remind Leo: 'Your secret weapon is learning'.

These aren't just nice thoughts. They are daily reminders for both of us: to live with joy, trust our instincts and keep growing. Ultimately, I know that the values I pass on to my children today will resonate with them even after they have grown up.

> It's not just about my words, it's also about how I live them.

This too is part of Intentional Parenting.

We teach best by example and my mission is to be a courageous and generous mum, raising Viola and Leonardo with care and love, encouraging them to be curious, free and happy for no reason.

Does it require commitment?

Yes. Of course. It takes a lot of effort to avoid reacting impulsively, and to start becoming aware of the kind of parents we want to be for our children.

TAKEAWAYS

1. **There is nothing to fix**, and no one to fix: **there is no perfect way to be a parent.**

2. **Intentionality is a matter of choice**: some people bring children into the world because they have always wanted to, others because it just happens. But you are born an intentional parent when you choose to be one, in your own unique way.

3. **When does a parent come into being?** When you start to choose how to raise your children and make sure that your actions are in line with your goals.

3/ It Starts with Us

QUESTION: Have you ever felt like you were in a tragicomic film and couldn't figure out whether you liked it or not?

SPOILER: It's your film, if it's not working, rewrite it.

Let's go back to the noodle scene from a few pages ago: the restaurant is full, and your son starts eating with his hands.

Everyone is watching him (of course, the restaurant is very crowded) and you feel mortified.
People will think that you haven't been able to teach your son good manners.
And so you get angry and put him in his place.
A good ticking off is what he needs, you think.

Besides, you're not only doing it for his own good (*because you don't eat with your hands and good manners are important!*), but your reaction is also much more 'soft and modern' than your parents' would have been.
That's what you're thinking, angry parent.

Personal identity

As parents, we often think about what we want for our children - their happiness, their success and their good manners - but we don't always stop to think about our personal identity.

So, what's this 'personal identity' then?

In a nutshell, it is what makes us who we are. Identity is the way we see ourselves and those around us; it is the way we behave when nobody is watching; it is what shapes our universe in a unique way, literally and concretely giving form to our world.

More than any other aspect, it is what shapes our specific map of the world (we'll talk about this in *beacon* 6), that is, the filter through which we see and perceive everything we experience.

Among other things, identity tells us what is important to us and what is not. It establishes priorities and boundaries.

A simple example? Being tidy.

For some people it's so important that if they find something lying around - a pair of shoes out of place, a toy on the floor, even cutlery upside down in the dishwasher - they risk a panic attack. For others, the problem doesn't even exist. It doesn't even arise.

I have a friend who lives with a partner and a long-haired dog (a Czechoslovakian Wolfdog). Neither of them, despite being subject to gravity, really notices the floor, and since the dog loses hair and her partner doesn't pick it up, my friend regularly finds the floor in a terrible state when she gets home. The odd thing is, the rest of the house is spotless: everything clean and tidy, except the floor.

It's important to her and that's why she notices it.

For him the floor is something he understands on a rational level (he knows there's a surface on which dust and hairs settle), but it's beyond his conscious sphere, so he ignores it. And this isn't because he's bad, or doesn't care about having a tidy house, but because his identity has different priorities. In other words, it matters to her, but not to him.

The things that matter to us form our identity. But they are not immutable, on the contrary, they change with us. Especially when we become parents.

Suddenly, our decisions no longer concern only us, but also our children, who depend on us to feed, protect and guide them. After forty weeks of waiting, the baby is born, and we immediately go into 'survival' mode: struggling with something completely new, as magnificent as it is frightening.

They're tiny! They're fragile. They're incomprehensible!
They don't talk.
Why do they cry? Are they hungry? Sleepy?
Or could it be teething, colic, a virus?
What if it's a virus?

The weeks go by and the babies grow.

You only have to leave the house for a couple of hours to see how much, and how quickly.

They start to move, get up, crawl, run, start to talk. They fall, get up again.

They throw tantrums, the 'why why why' starts. You turn away for a moment and they're already at the nursery.

Here come the friends, separation anxiety, cosmic dramas. And then homework and 'I want a mobile phone because everyone has one except me'.

Five minutes and they are talking gibberish, ignoring you, arguing with you and are already ready to choose secondary school.

Another ten and they're at university.

Yes, for me too, the first weeks after giving birth were in 'survival' mode and it took me a while to have time to see the opportunity that was unfolding before me: being an intentional parent could shape the kind of person I would raise. And, thanks to her, the world.

Sounds good on paper, doesn't it?

Don't think I don't know that as they grow and the going gets tough, our children test us in ways we never expected: are we as patient as we'd like to be? Are we consistent? Are we fun?

Every day as a parent is a day full of decisions and choices. Non-stop. From dawn to dusk and often even in between. And it's easy, in the midst of the thousand commitments in our lives, to let ourselves be overwhelmed and forget, for a moment, what really matters to us.

Every decision we make as parents is a reflection of our identity. The same goes for every action and reaction. Every time we enforce a rule, offer encouragement or say 'no', we are not only teaching our child, but we are also defining who we are as parents.

Still on the subject of identity, let's think about rules. Reflecting on our personal identity helps us as parents to choose rules in a more intentional way.

FEW RULES, CLEAR AND ALIGNED

We don't need more rules, we need fewer, because fewer rules means more intentionality.

It's not about being too permissive or too strict, but about being *intentional*: *choosing* what really matters to us. And, still talking about choices, it's important that ours are clear and aligned with who we really are.

For me, these rules have always been few and *adamantine*, clear and resistant just like diamonds: respect family meals, be punctual and keep promises.

For example, before becoming a parent, punctuality was one of the values of my personal identity. And in fact, as a parent, it has become something that I consciously want to instil in my children. I wanted (and want) them to understand that being punctual goes beyond arriving on time - it shows respect, responsibility, and keeping promises.

In one word, it's *integrity*.

The rules for my children have never been just rules, they are a reflection of who I am and what I wanted to pass on.

I know that as parents it's easy to get caught up in everyday life and lose sight of the big picture. That's why we rarely stop to think about who we are, what has brought us here, to reflect on our values and our habits. Maybe we don't like some things, but we accept them as part of who we are.

The point is that reflecting helps us see that everything starts with us, and that's a luxury, because when we stop to think, we might discover that we are not who we want to be.

And that's why this *beacon* is called 'It all starts with us': parenting should focus on us rather than on our children (otherwise it would be called *childing*). Only after taking a look inside ourselves can we positively influence our parenting style.

Everyone has their own, as we said.

> There is no standard style, and there is no perfect style.

Every parent can find their own, even when it goes against the opinions of others.

For example, since the birth of my first daughter, Viola, my husband and I have made a somewhat radical and decidedly 'unpopular' choice: we have decided to erase the no's.

Yes, you read that correctly!

What do you mean, 'erase the no's'?

Now, before you imagine my house as some kind of hell ruled by my children, let me explain. We knew that many experts, educators and parents with the best intentions are convinced that children absolutely need 'no's'. For them, no's are the only way for children to learn to respect boundaries and distinguish right from wrong. However, we had the feeling that it wasn't the only one. And that there

49

was another one, even better.

And guess what? New flash: 'no' is not the only way! Think about it: how do you feel when someone constantly tells you what not to do? Do you like it? Probably not, because 'no' breaks the relationship.

Nobody likes to be told 'no'. Who wants to hear 'no' and 'don't' all day long? But wait. Our choice to consciously avoid 'no' never meant letting my daughter run wild. It wasn't about ignoring limits or saying 'yes' to everything. Far from it! It was about turning the script around and focussing on the positive.

Instead of 'Don't touch the vase!', we chose to say: 'Let's put the vase on the shelf where it will be safe'.

Instead of 'Don't run in the house!', we said: 'Let's walk around here like panthers on tip-toes and then go outside to run!'.

See the difference? It's subtle, but powerful. It's about guiding, not forbidding. It's about empowering, not limiting. Now, let's be clear: it takes practice. It's easy to fall back into the 'no' trap, especially when we're stressed, tired, a nanosecond away from collapsing into sleep. But it's worth it.

So, how did we deal with the real 'nos'?

We reserved them for the really important things: safety, growth and other absolutely necessary aspects. Things like: 'No, I won't let you do that, it's not safe' or 'No, you can't have a phone yet, you are not ready'. These 'no's carried weight because they were rare and well calibrated. And here's the beauty of it: we never used a 'no' that we weren't ready to respect.

No empty threats, no wishy-washy 'no's' that turn into 'okay, fine' five minutes later. Kids are incredibly clever. They know when we're bluffing. If we say 'no' it has to be for real, and whenever we can, we abandon the 'no's', focus on the positives and offer them alternatives.

Okay, that sounds great, but what can we do when our children resist?

When this happens, one of the most difficult parts of parenting is enforcing the rules, and this is exactly when loving firmness comes into play.

It's about maintaining our position with empathy, combining consistency with connection.

Let me tell you a story.

Recently, a friend told me about a battle with his three-year-old. The child wanted ice cream before lunch and when he was told no, the tantrum that followed was epic. But instead of losing his temper, my friend remained calm. 'I know you really want ice cream and I understand, it's delicious!' - but he didn't change the rule. 'Ice cream comes after lunch,' he repeated several times. He didn't raise his voice or lose his patience. He maintained a warm tone and a firm approach. In the end, the storm passed and the rule was respected.

So, the next time we find ourselves enforcing one of our few clear and aligned rules, let's take a moment to reflect on what they say about our identity.

Perhaps they relate to respect, responsibility or the importance of family time.

Whatever they are, let's remember that we are not only raising a child, but we are living our values. And in doing so, we are creating a legacy of love, connection and intention. The bottom line is, it all comes down to self-awareness.

TAKEAWAYS

1. **Everything starts with us**: being a parent means raising human beings, while expressing who we truly are.

2. **Do you know who you are?** Pause to reflect on your actions, which speak louder than words, and ask yourself if your behavior is in line with your identity.

3. **Few rules, few 'no's', a lot of clarity and always consistency:** you don't need a thousand rules, it's better to have fewer as long as they are clear, solid, and in line with the kind of parent you want to be.

4/ INSIDE-OUT

QUESTION: How do I stay calm when my children drive me crazy?

SPOILER: When you become aware of your emotions and how they work, you can start to respond with increasing intentionality.

Imagine that for Lucy it's a very unpleasant morning, light brown in colour, to be clear. One of those where the alarm clock doesn't go off, you spill coffee on yourself and you've also stepped on a LEGO in the corridor. All this by half seven in the morning.

And now, in this lovely scene, the youngest child is insisting (yelling) that he wants to go to nursery in his pyjamas.

'Pyjamas pyjamas pyjamas!'

And the older one, eight years old and with the voice of a soprano, is furious because she can't find her red T-shirt with the little stars on it.

'Mummyyyyy, where did you put my T-shirt?'

'I don't know, darling, I'll be right there'.

The T-shirt is in the wash. Lucy looks for an alternative among a pile of other T-shirts (on the floor) taller than her.

'The pink one with the little stars, the same-same-identical one?'

The older one doesn't want to hear about it: it's creased. The younger one doesn't want to hear about it either: he wants his pyjamas with the backstitch. As usual, time flies and the three of them are already late. Lucy counts to ten.

The older one keeps shouting and now says she won't go out without the red T-shirt. Ten is too few. She counts to 82, 83, 84, then she snaps because enough is enough...

KEEP CALM AND... DO YOU REALLY KNOW YOURSELF?

When asked to name the most difficult thing for man, the Greek philosopher Thales replied: 'To know oneself'.

Know oneself? Are we talking about self-awareness?

Let's clarify one thing right away: self-awareness is not introspection or meditation. It's not even mindfulness and it's not an innate talent. It's simply the ability to understand who we really are: who we think we are and how we think others see us. The first is internal self-awareness (inside), the second is external self-awareness (out).

The inside concerns us, our thoughts, feelings and reactions. The outside concerns the way we think others perceive us. Thinking about it is important because we may realise that inside and out are not very aligned: I think I'm easy going, but if you don't do what I say, watch out.

Psychologists Shelley Duval and Robert Wicklund define it as the ability to focus on oneself and to evaluate whether one's actions, thoughts or emotions are in line with one's internal standards.

If we break it down even further, self-awareness is the ability to recognise what is happening inside us - the emotional reactions triggered by events and our environment - and to learn to manage them.

*What happens when we lack
self-awareness?*

We risk operating on autopilot, and therefore reacting impulsively, and then feeling guilty and wondering why we reacted in a way we really don't like.

*Why is this important for us
as parents?*

Because every day we find ourselves facing situations that test us, challenging our limits, our patience, our values, our ability to lead our children.

'To lead'.

Being a parent is absolutely the highest form of leadership.

In its original meaning, the word *leader* actually means guide, the kind of person we hire to take us on a trek, to explore an unknown place and to get us to the top safely.

The guide knows the trails, and therefore knows which ones to take us on so we can enjoy the view and the adventure while he keeps us safe.

It's not enough for the guide to be an expert, they also need to be charismatic, pleasant, and able to anticipate possible dangers, reacting if they arise; it's clear that to succeed, a good guide must be hyper-aware of their emotions.

First of all, what emotions really are, and then how to manage them properly.

Are we talking about feelings?

Not really, because emotions are much more than feelings: they are our body's alarm system. Every time something happens, our brain gets to work and, through a series of *disambiguation* and predictions, prepares to react[3].

It disambiguates to literally[4] remove ambiguity from the event; it makes predictions about how things will turn out in order to save time and effort.

Instead of thinking of the brain as vague and mushy grey matter, let's imagine it as a *control tower*.

Now consider that this control tower coordinates more than 70 trillion collaborators (cells and bacteria), in a perpetual state of alert, each of which is always connected to all the others.

Emotions are not things that we happen to feel. And they are not innate, but constructed by our brain.

We don't just feel angry, or sad, or overjoyed.

Since we first appeared as a species on this planet, every emotion we feel has been created by our brain with a very specific purpose: to remove ambiguity from events in order to protect us from threats and recognise opportunities.

> » Threats such as a saber-toothed tiger, a wild animal, a new plant, an unknown path.

---

3   "How Emotions are Made: The Secret Life of the Brain", by Dr. Lisa Feldman Barrett, PhD, who is a University Distinguished Professor of Psychology at Northeastern University, and among the top 0.1% most cited scientists in the world for her revolutionary research in psychology and neuroscience.

4   To disambiguate is to make something perfectly clear by removing all uncertainty. Disambiguate is another way to say clarify, or clear up.

» Opportunities such as edible, tasty, juicy foods, and anything that helps us accumulate energy or not waste it in times of scarcity.

200,000 years ago, threats had sharp teeth; today they show up via WhatsApp in the parents' group chat, they have the voice of the Head Teacher calling us, the disapproving eyes of someone watching us with our kids.

The fact is that every time our brain perceives a threat, it triggers a series of reactions to put us on alert: it increases our heart rate, makes our palms sweat, and tenses our muscles.

And it does so by default, automatically.

The point is that the threat doesn't need to be real, or really relevant: the brain prefers to overreact, just in case. Since these reactions are automatic, we can't block them (and it wouldn't make any sense to try).

But here's the thing:

We can always:

» Become aware of what emotion we are feeling and why;
» Learn to control how we react to it.

The only thing we can control is our reaction. This is where self-awareness comes in, the bridge that connects our good intentions to intentionality.

> If we want to change something, we must first notice it, get to know it and recognise it, and then decide intentionally how to behave.

Also because our initial reaction depends largely on how our body feels at that precise moment, on what it is fighting internally, even when we don't know what is happening.

Being aware also allows us to recognise our *familiarity*

zones which, as we saw in *beacon* no. 1, could be anything but comfortable.

And here are the questions to ask ourselves.

What exactly are we feeling?

When we feel something strong, let's try to understand what emotion it is. Let's go into detail.

Asking ourselves what exactly we are feeling means giving a specific name to the emotion, and therefore helping ourselves to recognise it.

Why are we feeling it? How is our body?

Recent discoveries in neuroscience have shown that the variety and intensity of our emotions depend very much on how our body feels while we experience them (we'll talk more about this later).

Just think of the days when we seem to be more nervous, and just the smallest thing, a trivial nothing, is enough to set us off; on the other hand, sometimes we manage to handle half-catastrophes with the aplomb of a Tibetan monk.

The most Zen days are those in which our body isn't fighting any internal battle. No viruses, no cells going crazy, just heaven.

The others are when the control tower is busy: a fever, yoghurt that's expired recently... We don't realise it, but our brain does, and since it has no time to waste, it sets off all the alarms, often exacerbating the intensity of what it makes us feel.

What is the trigger that has set off this emotion? What is the thought that is generating it? Why are we reacting this way? What does this situation remind me of?

It could be a moment that recalls something else, perhaps unrelated to our children, or maybe we could find ourselves in a familiar situation. Instead of reacting automatically, we can become aware of what is happening in our body and in our thoughts, take a deep breath and instead of counting to ten, take a step to the side to respond in a more intentional way.

A step to the side?

We can imagine the *familiarity zone* as a circle around our feet that keeps us stuck.

'Seeing' the circle, that is, becoming aware of it, allows us to get out of it.

Since sometimes counting to ten doesn't help, we can try something new. For example, take a little step to the side, beyond the circle, and voilà, we're out of it.

This very simple movement will tell our 'control tower' that we are doing something new and, step by step, will help us transform the novelty into routine. It only takes a second to choose to behave differently.

What takes time is to get used to the new way.

The key point of this topic is that self-awareness allows us to choose, to make choices that are more in line with the kind of parent we want to be, with our identity, and also with that of our children.

In addition to helping us manage our emotions better, self-awareness also helps us shape our children's emotional intelligence.

How?

By showing them, through our actions, how to better manage their emotions. When we are self-aware parents, we are more likely to raise emotionally intelligent children, who are resilient and able to lead with empathy.

As we were saying, self-awareness is a skill, like any skill it is something we can learn and consolidate.

The aim? Always the same: to choose what kind of parents we want to be for our children.

TAKEAWAYS

1. **It all starts with us and self-awareness is a skill**: recognising what you feel is the first step in choosing how to react.

2. **Emotions don't just happen, they are constructed by your brain**: learning to recognise them helps you to choose how you want to react more consciously.

3. **Instead of using 'autopilot' mode,** when you recognise a familiarity zone, taking **a step to the side** helps you to 'leap' out of it.

5/ OUR COMPASS

QUESTION: What am I teaching my children? What really matters?

SPOILER: The values we instil today shape their tomorrow.

Viola's birthday falls just one day before International Women's Day. A few years ago, I gave her a magnificent book "Goodnight Stories for Rebel Girls[5]". I thought about how inspiring it would be for her to read stories of extraordinary women who defied societal expectations, followed their passions, and created significant changes for humanity. They all managed to follow their dreams with courage and determination.

The following day, as I flipped through the pages, it dawned on me that these stories were not only important for Viola, but equally, if not more so, for Leo. He, too, needed to learn about the women who changed the world, to remember their names, and to understand the impact and change they brought.

At the same time, I also thought about how we usually talk about a certain type of males: strong, warrior-like, conquerors, heroes, explorers. If our storytelling excludes women, and fixates on a singular masculine archetype—the stoic, the unyielding, the emotionally reticent (for emotions are, after all, 'girl stuff')—how can we expect to raise individuals who embody, rather than merely discuss, gender equality?

This sparked a deeper inquiry: how do modern, empowered women cultivate a narrative shift within their children?

Over the years, these reflections have sharpened my understanding of my parental role: to consciously

---

5   Good Night Stories for Rebel Girls: 100 tales of extraordinary women', Elena Favilli, Particular Book, 2017

shape the individuals I'm raising, and to consider their future impact on the world.

Through the stories I share, I transmit my core values and aspirations for them. I yearn for them to embody respect, courage, integrity, and consistency. I desire this for them today, in the everyday, and for their future, knowing that present actions resonate far beyond the immediate.

Do you remember when I said my mission is to change the world through my children?

Here's the point.

The leaders, the innovators, the true architects of tomorrow's change are moulded by the values we instil today. What we impart to our children today not only shapes their character but also the world they will inhabit. If we desire a future founded on kindness, integrity, and respect, we must raise children who embody these principles.

We don't necessarily have to talk explicitly about values, especially when our children are young. As we explored in *beacon* no. 2, we can employ a more subtle tool: mottos.

Mottos?

These are little phrases, encapsulating a concept, a belief, an aspiration, or an attitude—a personal mantra that fuels both us and our children.

Mottos can be a powerful source of encouragement during challenging times, reminding our children of their strengths, their 'superpowers'.

Each time I remind Viola that 'The important thing is to have fun' and Leonardo that 'Your secret weapon is learning', I'm not merely offering nice thoughts; I'm providing them with frameworks for joyful living, trusting their instincts, and embracing continuous growth. Whenever I urge Leo to be kind, to listen, or to champion what's right, I know I'm nurturing a person who will make a tangible difference: a person who leads with empathy, treats others with respect and understands that true strength comes from character, not control.

What do I want for him?

I want Leo to be a confident child today, and at the same time, free to express his emotions.

Speaking of emotions, once again, I'm teaching him to express them, to give them a specific name, and to self-regulate.

For example, when he feels upset or worried, I help him to define what he is feeling and then, by showing him that frustration and sadness are not weaknesses, I act as a role model and help him to regulate his emotions.

I don't block them. I don't minimise them. I don't make fun of him. By doing this, he is learning that true strength lies in self-awareness and empathy.

• Self-awareness: understanding what we feel, naming our emotions, realising that the brain is ours and because it is ours, we can make it work for us (and not against us).

• Empathy: understanding how others feel, and therefore putting ourselves in their shoes.

I also make sure that he understands respect, not only as a rule but as the basis of every relationship.

For example, when he speaks in an unkind way, :

- I remember not to react impulsively;
- I help him recognise what he's feeling, by giving a name to his emotions;
- With clear and intentional language (we'll talk about this shortly), I gently and firmly remind him. 'This is not how we treat each other'.

In this way I help him shape his reactions, develop emotional intelligence and resilience.

Every day, in every choice we make, our effort as parents transmits values that will resonate in the future.

In the chaos of daily life, it's easy to forget why we do what we do.

But the point is this: the difference between being the best parent we can be and being intentional about it brings us back to our values.

Our values are what really matters to us.

While reflecting on how we parent, let's ask ourselves:

> » What do we really care about?

> » Which values do we want to prioritise?

> » How do we want to behave with our children?

> » Which guiding principles do we want to pass on?

These values are our compass. And the answers will shape the way we approach every aspect of our parenting journey.

TAKEAWAY

1. **The values we give our children today shape their tomorrow:** if you want a future built on kindness, integrity and respect, you must raise children who live these values.

2. **Children are sponges:** to pass on your values, you can use stories, mottos and facts. When you act as role models for patience, empathy and respect, you give your children the opportunity to become extraordinary adults, truly capable of making our world a better place.

3. **Values: your compass.** Knowing and recognising your values helps you make increasingly intentional choices, even and especially when the going gets tough.

6/ THROUGH THEIR EYES

QUESTION: Why doesn't my child understand, listen to me, see what's obvious, etc., etc.?

SPOILER: Because their world is not yours.

«Alice: Would you tell me, please, which way I ought to go from here?

The Cheshire Cat: That depends a good deal on where you want to get to.
Alice: I don't much care where.
The Cheshire Cat: Then it doesn't much matter which way you go.
Alice: ... As long as I get somewhere.

The Cheshire Cat: Oh, you're sure to do that, if you only walk long enough».

– Lewis Carroll – Alice in Wonderland

Alice walks and walks. She doesn't care where she's going: she just keeps going. Her journey in Wonderland is reminiscent of the way many of us approach parenthood.

Among the thousand things to do and think about, we may find ourselves going down our path without a destination: one day after another, six or seven commitments at a time.

Mind you: going on an adventure – wandering – can be wonderful. It can surprise us, and even take us to fantastic places. But sometimes it can keep you circling rather than moving forward.

What if, instead of wandering, we chose a direction?

Intentional Parenting is exactly that: a direction. It's still a journey, but suddenly it's a journey with a *vision*[6], that is, seeing our goal and our purpose.

We already know this, don't we?

Like so many other things that we know very well but find it hard to put into practice, and this is simply because we fill our days with things to do.

We are busy, most of the time.

We are too busy to think about why we do the things we do.

And since we are busy, and our days are full, we think we are doing our best and being effective.

Are we really?

Like Alice, if we continue to do what we are doing, even at our best, we believe that sooner or later, we will get somewhere. But do we ever ask ourselves if we are going in OUR direction?

Are we doing useful things, the kind of things that take us where we really want to go?

'It depends a lot on where you want to get to', says the Cheshire Cat, who then adds:

'I'm not crazy. My reality is just different from yours'.

It really is, and it is for everyone.

With much less philosophy than Lewis Carroll and his Cheshire Cat, the truth is that each of us is the centre of our own world, as if to say that each of us has a *map of the*

---

6   Vision comes from the Latin 'Vision', with a deep sense of direction and purpose. Vision from the Latin 'visio-onis', derived from videre- 'to see'.

world[7] that is entirely our own and different from any other map.

Remember when we were talking about identity and I told you about my friend's partner who couldn't see the floor? Well, that's it.

Each person has a different perspective from all the others.

If a spilled glass of milk seems trivial to us, it can be monumental for a child. A real tragedy. In the same way, what we see as our new silk shirt stained forever, for our little Frida Kahlo and the young Da Vinci is a masterpiece worthy of a museum.

For everyone, always, what counts is our perception, that is, the map with which our brain represents reality.

A representation, therefore.

Not reality.

If we think of the map of a city, one of those vintage ones made of paper, which we never knew how to fold, it is clear that we are not looking at the real city, only a representation of it.

This image shows us that the map is not reality, nor is it the territory.

Let's go back to the city map and look at it carefully. There are the main landmarks, the roads, the parks, the streets, the rivers, etc. Yet, it's clear that it's not the city because the map

---

7   The *map of the world* is a concept developed by Richard Bandler (psychologist and co-creator of NLP, also known as Neuro-Linguistic Programming) who explains how our understanding of the world doesn't depend on reality, but rather on the internal map that each of us draws by putting together ideas, beliefs, concepts, experiences, and preconceptions.

is just a map. If we look at the street where our favourite baker is, we don't smell the bread. There are no tourists in the square, no runners in the parks.

Obvious, isn't it?

And this is because the map is a simplified version of reality. Just as our personal map simplifies the world around us.

THE MAP IS NOT THE TERRITORY

The map is a tool[8], shaped by what our brain has chosen to include, exclude or distort. When drawing our map, the brain simplifies experiences and generalises in order to save energy.

Each of us constructs our own map of the world from the moment we are born, drawing it from everything we have seen, heard, felt and learnt. Over time, this map becomes our world. Here's something else. Compared to the city analogy, when we talk about human beings, no two maps are identical.

Each person's map is unique, just like their fingerprint. And this also applies to our children.

One of the fundamental differences is that while our maps are relatively complete, those of our children are still a work in progress, barely sketched in.

In this context, something that we see as dangerous might not be so in their eyes; something that for us is easy might seem difficult, insurmountable, or even impossible, in their eyes.

What may seem instinctive, logical, even obvious to us, may not necessarily be so for them.

For us, a puddle is a nuisance. And for them?
For us, doing homework is very important. And for them?
For us, 'being home before midnight' is protection.
And for a teenager?

---

8   This concept, 'the map is not the territory' was first introduced by Alfred Korzybski at the beginning of the 20th century, and reminds us that the way we perceive and interpret reality is shaped by our personal experiences, our beliefs and our assumptions.

Recognising the unique maps of our children helps us understand that nothing can be taken for granted. In parenting, this concept changes the game, also because it's easy to think that children 'should' see the world as we do.

Why doesn't Lucy care that her room is a mess?

Why doesn't Alice run to the table when I call her?

Why would Robert rather be crucified than do his homework?

Why doesn't Sam realise that I am on call and scream like a banshee?

Why doesn't Thomas even try?

Because Lucy, Alice, Robert, Sam and Thomas see things differently from us. In different ways. And with different results.

Why? Simply because they are not like us: they were born in a different world from ours (remember when we talked about generations?), and what's more, their maps are still being drawn. And here, once again, awareness helps us to choose. Instead of reacting on impulse, or on autopilot, when their behavior confuses us, we can stop and ask ourselves: 'What will their eyes see now?'

This change in mindset opens the door to a deeper connection, teaching us and at the same time our children empathy and humility.

What does humility have to do with it?

It's all about empathy, the core of the matter, and the key to every human relationship.

Speaking of maps, although much older than theirs, ours is not perfect either, which means there is always room to learn, to adjust, to add new reference points. And when we embrace this mentality, we provide our children with a model of flexibility and open-mindedness.

In practice, paying attention to 'their world' gets us used to looking beyond the surface, and to understanding rather than taking things for granted. It allows us to see the world with and through their eyes. And from there, we can start building a bridge to them, brick by brick.

TAKEAWAYS

1. **Every world is different because every map is different.** Each of us builds our own from the moment we are born, drawing it from everything we have seen, heard, felt and learnt. Over time, this map becomes our world.

2. **The map is not the territory,** it is only a representation, so there is no single 'truth'.

3. **Choosing to see their world helps you looking beyond the surface** and opens you up to empathy and connection.

7/ Our Inner Script

QUESTION: How can I do it when I already know I can't?

SPOILER: Everything you think is created by your brain, and since the brain is yours, make it play for you, not against you.

Mike is in the gym and is staring at the high bar. It's his turn to jump, grab the bar and pull himself up. He takes a deep breath, looks at the metal again and doesn't move. A conversation is taking place in his head.

'You'll never make it'.

'Your arms are like two sticks'.

'You're not strong enough'.

The coach waits. She doesn't move either.

'You'll be rubbish, you wimp,' continues the voice in Mike's head, which has the same mocking tone as the bullies. The same inflection, identical.

Meanwhile, the queue starts to murmur.

'We haven't got all day!'

Then the coach turns around, glares at the people who expressed their unsolicited opinion, and then turns to Mike.

'You can do it. You know you can, you just need to want it'.

Mike takes a step back and tells the coach that he really doesn't feel like it.

'I don't feel ready'.

'At least try...' she tells him, thinking that this will give him the push he needs.

But he had already disappeared at the back of the group, his eyes lowered and his morale even lower.

If you now think that Mike is a child struggling with a pull-up that is too difficult for him, you should know that Mike is not 11 years old, but 42. He is a biochemist who loves reading and solving Sudoku, but as far as sport is concerned, he has always believed that he wasn't cut out for it.

And here's the point. Mike is an adult, and what he is experiencing now happens at every age.

Inside our beautiful little heads, there is a voice that accompanies us day by day, for each of the 14, 15, 16 hours we spend awake. And that voice doesn't always play on our team.

Quite the opposite, in fact: all too often this inner chatter works against us. Once again, the responsibility lies with our brain. It's constantly trying to keep us alive, and to do so, it needs to conserve energy—by simplifying as much as possible and following the same old patterns.

If we tell ourselves that we're not good at jumping, the brain accepts it. In fact, it accepts it as truth and from then on avoids making any effort. It does this for our own good, for our safety, and to save our skin, as if we were still surrounded by Jurassic dangers.

The problem is that we are often not aware of how our inner language can influence our emotions and our actions.

The brain is not lazy, as we said, and it is not even stubborn: it is just efficient, at least from its point of view. And yet, precisely because of its Sheldon Cooper-like efficiency (yes, the theoretical physicist from The Big Bang Theory) we can make it work in our favour.

If we tell ourselves that we are adaptable and that we will succeed, the same thing happens: the brain believes it for the simple fact that our mind (it's now proven) doesn't distinguish between reality and imagination.

Now, let's think about our role as parents.

Every day we face hundreds of unexpected events, difficult moments, and small or big crises: if we tell ourselves that we are not good at handling events, our brain will believe us.

But what if we change the story?

If we start to tell ourselves that we are learning to react intentionally, our mind will help us to become more intentional parents.

This switch works not only for us, but also for our children, who are sponges with a PhD in observation and replication. They absorb everything: the things we do and even the way we talk to ourselves. They see it, they hear it and they learn from it. And this is our emotional identity: our inner 'script', made up of everything we say to our brain. In other words: what we think. Whatever we tell it, our brain is forced to respond.

'Remember, it's your body, your brain'.
Richard Bandler

Recognising that our thoughts are the basis of many of our emotions allows us to start questioning them, modifying the former to manage the latter with ease.

This applies to us and to our children.

By teaching them to question their inner voice and, if necessary, rewrite the script, we give them the tools to face the inevitable ups and downs of life.

Even though we have already introduced the topic of 'emotions', let's now try to go a little deeper.

EMOTIONS

Let's start with the term 'emotion', which comes from the French èmotion, which in turn derives from the Latin emovere, made up of:

'e'- (variant of ex-) = 'out';

'movere' = to move.

Looking at the etymological root, we see that through movement something intangible like an emotion becomes visible, and therefore physical, definitely material.

While human thinkers have always wondered about the origin of emotions, over time two macro-schools of thought have emerged, both part of the Classical Theory of Emotions:

• one that supports the existence of basic emotions common to all;

• the other that interprets emotions not as biologically determined entities but as social constructs.

Every theory on emotions tries to address three main questions.

1. The physical effects of emotions, such as the heart beating wildly or the skin sweating, activated by the autonomic nervous system (and therefore beyond our control).

2. The mental aspect of emotions (for example when we recognise what we feel and give it a name).

3. The variability of emotions, or rather the fact that they change, can evolve and sometimes disappear before we even realise it.

As we said in the 'inside-out' *beacon*, emotions can be perceived differently (with more or less intensity) both depending on the state of our body when we feel them, and depending on the name we give them.

Let's start with the body.

We've said that the body influences emotions. Depending on what happens inside us, emotions can vary: they can be perceived as more or less positive. Body and mind are one, right?

I feel fear and start to tremble.
I feel embarrassed and blush.
Anxiety makes my stomach turn...

The realisation that what we feel can also depend on our physical state helps us in various ways.

It helps us to evaluate our emotions and those of others with greater empathy.

It allows us to act to modify our perception of emotions, through the body, that is, through our posture and movements.

Posture? Movements? In what sense?

Since the body influences emotions, if we act on the body, we modify the emotions.

Is this possible?

From the roots of the word, we see that emotions are deeply linked to something we can control: movement. And this is because our body speaks.

Let me tell you a story.

One day, during a conference, a client went to say goodbye to his mental coach, telling him that he was extremely worried because his thirteen-year-old daughter kept fainting. 'Every time we go to church, she faints'. After the first fainting episode, the parents took their daughter to the hospital, but everything turned out to be fine. They returned home and the following Sunday, before going to church, the girl started to get agitated. 'I'm afraid of fainting again', she told her parents. Her father talked to her, she felt better and the family went to mass. But as soon as they arrived at the church, the girl fainted again. After telling the story, the father asked the coach why this was happening and what he could do to help his daughter. 'Are you sure she wants to come to mass?'

'Yes, of course. She's always been happy to come,' replied the father, continuing, 'she's never rebelled and never told us she didn't want to come with us. But I don't understand why she keeps fainting. Could it be that she does it on purpose?'

'Your daughter doesn't faint on purpose; even if she has never told you and perhaps she is not even aware of it, her body reacts, and makes a decision for her'.

'And what can I do to help her? For me it is important that she prays...'

'Then let her be free to choose the way she wants to pray'.

The girl's body had chosen to speak for her, expressing what she felt without ever having said it out loud.

This story reminds us of something fundamental: our emotions are not just *abstract feelings*, but are phenomena with physical manifestations and very concrete effects.

Emotions are more real than reality itself!

And, in fact, here's the key: just as our emotions shape our body's reactions, at any given moment, we can choose to influence our emotions through our actions.

For example, I tell my kids: 'When you feel an emotion you don't like, go in front of the mirror, put on your biggest, goofiest smile, and stand there for thirty seconds'.

With a face like that, it's inevitable that you'll start to laugh[9] and this will trigger an extra production of feel-good hormones. Obviously, it doesn't erase the unpleasant emotion forever, but it instantly changes the way you perceive it. And it's good for the mind, for our thoughts, and even for our health, as has been proven by studies in the field of gelotology (the study of laughter and its effects on the body, from a psychological and physiological perspective).

Let's talk about names

We all express our emotions in different ways. So much so that some people even have additional emotions.

These include the Japanese word *amae* (the emotion we feel when someone takes care of us); the Finnish *kaukokaipuu* (nostalgia for a place we have never been); and the New Guinea *awumbuk* (the melancholy that follows the departure of a beloved guest).

---

9   Laughing increases adrenaline and dopamine, which in turn releases natural 'morphines', endorphins, and enkephalins. Endorphins reduce pain and tension, allowing you to reach a state of relaxation and tranquillity. Encephalins seem to boost the immune system, helping it to fight disease better. At the same time, further down, they increase the production of another hormone, serotonin (95% produced by the intestinal microbiota).

Why are we talking about names? After all, they're just words...

True, yet the words we use, with others and with ourselves, don't just describe what we feel, but give shape to our reality. They tell it. They draw it. They make it real.

And since we should remember by now that our brain simplifies, many people tend to reduce emotions to just a few macro-categories: happiness, sadness, anger, fear.

But happy how? Bursting with joy?

And sad? In what sense? Sad with nostalgia, or sad with a broken heart? Sad because of disappointment, regret, remorse, loss?

Nuances matter because giving emotions an appropriate name helps us to frame[10] them. In practice, it clarifies them, removing their ambiguity of meaning.

Language defines experiences, gives them form, makes them tangible. The more specific it is, the more useful it is to us.

The language we choose to use doesn't just describe the world: it creates it.

'When you lack the words to describe what you feel, you live with frustration'.
Vera Gheno[11]

What we tell ourselves is what we experience.

And this is because our brain listens to us and aligns itself

10   To explore a little more deeply the vast universe of human emotions, as many as 87, I recommend 'Atlas of the Heart: Mapping Meaningful Connection and the Language of Human Experience' by Brené Brown.

11   Vera Gheno, linguist, author of 'Grammamanti. Immaginare futuri con le parole', Norberto Bobbio Editore, April 2024.

with what we tell it. For better or for worse.

For our brain, reality doesn't matter: only how we tell it does. Just think of the placebo effect and its evil twin, the incredible but now well-established 'nocebo effect'.

Studies have proven that whatever you tell your brain, it works.

For better or, unfortunately, for worse.

> » Placebo effect: you take a drug that you believe to be powerful and you immediately feel better. The drug is water and sugar, with zero active ingredients, yet it works. The shocking thing is that you don't even need to think that the drug is powerful: suggestion works even when they tell you that what you are taking is a placebo.

> » Nocebo effect: they tell you that you have or might have a disease and from that moment on you really do have it. All the symptoms, down to the last one[12].

This, besides being mind-blowing, is an opportunity for us and for our children.

Intentionally choosing what we tell ourselves helps us and them become increasingly aware of the connection between body and mind.

It leads us to realise that we are not at the mercy of events.

It shows us that whatever happens to us, we can always choose how to react.

---

12   Placebo and Nocebo, from the articles of Dr Francesco Fratto, pharmacist and Gut Brain Coach who deals with body and mind wellness, microbiota, meditation and neuroscience. On Substack: francescofratto. substack.com

'Remember that it's your body and your brain.
You are not a victim of the universe, you are the
universe'.
Richard Bandler

And this is an incredibly powerful awareness because the more we become aware of the body-brain connection, thought and actions, the more we can guide not only our emotions, but also help our children, our loved ones and the people around us navigate their emotional world with greater ease and confidence.

TAKEAWAYS

1. **What you choose to tell yourself must work for you, not against you. Since the brain is yours**, you can always choose to tell it things that help you, and in doing so you will not only help yourself but also your children.

2. **Emotions arise from thought:** when you change the thought, you change the emotion.

3. **The way you describe it to yourself is how you experience it**: giving emotions an appropriate name helps you become aware of them and therefore choose how to react with increasing intentionality.

8/ THE BRIDGE

QUESTION: How do I get them to listen to me?

SPOILER: With trust, a *dream house* that you can build.

Until yesterday, Laura and Simone's son was good, polite, kind, cheerful, talkative, very affectionate, super obedient. Then, suddenly, the chatter disappeared, as did the hugs and kisses, and conversations became battles. Now, when Laura and her partner try to talk to Joe, they come up against a brick wall. He snaps and immediately attacks: 'You don't understand!' He disputes every single sentence and doesn't let anything slide.

The problems begin, and the two decide to change their approach. They try stricter rules, they ground him, they try to make themselves heard by raising their tone and their voice, and they don't give up, but Joe withdraws even more.

When they come to see me, Laura and Simone wonder if their Joe has really left, if it's adolescence or if it's their fault, that they aren't strict enough, rigid enough. In one question, Laura and Simone want to know if it's too late.

With different words and an equally different story, Paula also asks me the same thing. Unlike Joe, her daughter has always been a rebel, ever since she was little: a little pest with chubby cheeks and clever eyes. Already in primary school, Sophia began to question every single rule, and now that she is almost 15, Paula is starting to get seriously worried. She doesn't listen to her, she answers in monosyllables, she's not interested in anything concerning the family, the house, her future, let alone studying. She stays up late, glued to her phone, and of course in the morning she's a zombie. Making her do her homework, or even just go to school, is torture. She has already failed a subject and she doesn't know what to do anymore. When Paula asks for my help, she tells me she has tried everything.

Intentional Parenting is based on choice.

That's the whole point: choosing which parent we want to be, rather than doing our best, going a bit randomly like Alice in Wonderland (see *beacon* n.6).

To raise our children, to guide them and make sure they listen to us, finally and/or once again, we need connection and connection is based on trust.

Trust is the *bridge* between us and our children, and it is a *safe home*, where we all feel good.

It is the *bridge* that connects us to them, linking our good intentions to their world.

It's the *house* where we feel really at ease, it's where we always know we can return, because its gates are always open. Always. And because, inside, we feel so good.

It's a dream house, isn't it?

When our children are very young, they trust us almost blindly. We are their world, their heroes, their safe space. As they grow older, they start to question everything, including us. That's how it works: as the years go by, the picture becomes more and more complex.

Some sooner and some later, our children start to challenge

us and when faced with change, many of us try to tighten our grip: 'You have to do this and that because that's just the way it is'. For a while it works, at least until... it doesn't work anymore.

Trust is the basis of any human relationship, and as parents it is the key to building meaningful relationships. It is the magic ingredient that transforms 'because I say so' into 'I understand'.

When our children grow up and start to make their own decisions, there is no need to shout.

There's no need to insist that they obey us.

It's not necessary for them to fear us, and in fact it doesn't help.

What we need is for them to trust us. That is, for them to always know that every single thing we tell them makes sense, is useful, is coherent, is true, and works.

When we learn to build trust, they listen to us very carefully, what we say carries weight for them. I use the verb 'build' in line with the house analogy. A safe, solid, pleasant house to live in, supported by three pillars and with a fantastic atmosphere. The three pillars are:

1. coherence
2. presence
3. reciprocity.

The atmosphere is one of fun, like an extra bonus that makes us love the house we are building, that strengthens it, solidifies it and makes it the kind of house each of us would like to live in.

CONSISTENCY

Consistency is fundamental: we always keep our promises and make sure that our words are aligned with our actions and behavior.

If we say we'll be there, we make sure we are.

If we say we'll do something, we make sure we do it.

If we say we believe in a value, we make sure our children see it put into practice.

Our actions speak.

What if I make a mistake? What if I said I would do something and then I can't do it?

Sometimes it happens. Even with the best of intentions, we can all fail to keep our word. We promised we would go to their game, but then we get stuck in the office or in traffic. When this occurs, just apologise. Admitting our 'missteps' helps them understand that the unexpected is part of life and that everyone, including us, makes mistakes.

And when they do (make mistakes), resist the urge to correct them. If they say, 'I hate school,' make them feel heard, not judged.

'School is really tough right now, huh?'

This helps them feel understood. It shows that we are listening and recognising how they feel.

We also avoid immediate solutions. When they tell us about a problem, resist the urge to solve it right away.

Instead, say, 'That sounds difficult. Do you want to talk about it some more?'

Sometimes they just need to let off steam. Maybe they're not looking for solutions, just someone to listen to them.

PRESENCE

Let's do one thing at a time, properly, not six thousand things at once. Let's say goodbye to multitasking and when our children talk to us, let's focus on them. Let's put down the phone, make eye contact and show that they are the most important thing ever.

But what if I can't? What if it's the wrong time for me?

Then let's tell them: 'Is it urgent or is it OK if we talk about it in x minutes?'

It's always better to be clear than to pretend to listen to them while we continue to reply to emails...

RECIPROCITY

To build trust, we have to give it.

How? By showing that we trust them, for example, by giving them responsibilities in line with their age, and avoiding the hyper-control of nosey inquisitors. In other words, we respect their space and their privacy.

And when they make mistakes, because they will, we make sure we are their support, not their judge, helping them to learn from their mistakes.

FUN

To make our home a place of trust, to be listened to by our children and become the kind of parent we really want to be, let's value having fun. Let's have fun with our children, let's approach life with enthusiasm, cheerfulness and joy.

Let's celebrate our successes and theirs.

Sure, not everything is rosy, and we can't avoid the bad things, but we can learn to value the good ones more.

Let's laugh with them, even at ourselves. Let's learn to take ourselves a little less seriously, and a little more lightly.

And this is because the human brain learns through gratification. The pleasant, fun moments are the ones that stick with us and bring us closer to our children, from zero years to eighty-nine and beyond.

How can we build a house of trust?

One of the most powerful ways to build trust with our children is through 'rapport'.

Rapport is the ability to tune into our children's map of the world, so that they feel understood and safe, and therefore open up to us.

Rapport is a technique based on:

1. Listening. We listen with our ears, with our eyes, with our heart. We do it seriously, with all the attention we can muster, focussing on them, to really listen (we'll talk about this shortly, I promise).

2. Validation. We accept and welcome what they feel, even when we don't agree. We teach them to recognise emotions, we don't challenge them, and we don't minimise them. We value what they feel. We avoid judging them.

3. Frequencies and tuning. We understand their world, we

97

see their unique map, and we use their language in every way, with words, tones, posture, speed. We consciously use mirroring to put them at ease and tune in to their frequency. In the next chapter, we'll see how.

TAKEAWAYS

1. **Trust is the *bridge* between your good intentions and your children**. It is what transforms daily conversations into meaningful connections.

2. **Trust is a *house*** that stands on three pillars - consistency, presence, reciprocity - and in which there is a fantastic atmosphere of fun.

3. **To build the house of trust,** you need to use **rapport**: through listening, validation, and tuning in.

9/ The Frequency

QUESTION: It all sounds great, but it's like talking to a brick wall...

SPOILER: Find the frequency and - like magic - the wall will start to hear you.

Imagine you've just been given a really cool walkie-talkie as a gift and you invite Andrea to try it out. You go to the park and play a game of counting the number of people wearing fluorescent green T-shirts. You also decide that you 'were' Spiderman and Andrea 'was' Storm.

You position yourselves 300 metres apart. And you start the game. After a while you see the first green shirt and try to call Storm.

'Spider-Man calling Storm. Storm, come in!'

But Storm doesn't answer. And yet, the walkie-talkie is on. It goes *bzzz bzzz.*

Is it on?

You turn it off, then on again. *Yes. It's on.*

A second fluorescent T-shirt passes by, then a third and a fourth.

Each time, you try again, but nothing. Just bzzz bzzz. You press a few buttons at random. You look closely at the walkie-talkie and see a large wheel with little numbers on it. You try turning it this way and that but nothing happens. It just goes bzzz and that's it.

Meanwhile, here comes Storm from behind the bushes. He's waving his arms and shouting something at you. Too bad Storm is too far away for you to understand what he's saying...

In the end you give up and go to join Storm who, like you, has been trying to signal you with the fluorescent green t-shirts.

'It's not working' you tell him. But then Storm hands you his walkie-talkie and when you look at it closely, next to yours, you realise that his big wheel is on number five, yours on three.

This little walkie-talkie story is pretty basic, right? Yet every now and then (but sometimes too often) with our beloved children, we feel like we're talking to the wind. Or with walls.

At the same time, it also seems as if they don't speak the same language as us.

The topic we are about to explore in the next few pages is frequency, one of the three elements on which the rapport technique is based to build a house of trust.

As we said when talking about 'their world', each of us sees reality with our own eyes, through our own filters.

Being aware that their world is not ours, and that therefore their map is different, is the first step in tuning in to the right frequency, which is theirs.

It's about understanding their perspective, their priorities, and their unique way of both communicating and receiving messages. And then aligning our communication so that it gets through.

We humans start communicating right away. And we never stop doing it.

From the moment we're little more than a handful of cells immersed in our mother's amniotic fluid, we start receiving messages. And from that moment on, our mini-brain starts to show its preferences.

Even before we learn to talk, we express ourselves through sounds, facial expressions and movements. Then we say poo, mama, la-la-la (and here begins lallation) and finally we articulate our messages in an increasingly precise way.

We do it with and through words, and we continue to do

it with everything else.

Messages come to us and go out from us through three channels:

1.   Visual;
2.   Auditory;
3.   Kinaesthetic.

We use all three. But each of us has a favourite channel, that is, one that our brain likes best at a certain time and under certain conditions.

Again, both incoming and outgoing.

So, going back to the house of trust, to build it we must learn to tune in to the frequency of our children. And to do this, it helps if we are aware of which is the preferred channel at that specific moment.

I insist on specificity because preferences are not static, but dynamic. They change according to moments and situations. They change over time, and depending on how our brain classifies them.

THE VISUAL CHANNEL

It passes through sight, through the stimuli that come from the eyes. Those who are more sensitive to this channel are attracted to images, colours, shapes, to what they literally see. When communicating, they use phrases such as 'let me see', 'I saw that... you can see that...'

THE AUDITORY CHANNEL

It passes through hearing. It is the world of sounds, words, tone of voice, music. It is the favourite channel of those who say to us 'tell me'. 'Let's talk about it'. 'Tell me about it'.

It is the most loved by those who love stories, and podcasts. Those who make music. Those who write books.

Those who sing lullabies. And those who know lots of songs by heart.

THE KINAESTHETIC CHANNEL

This is the realm of movement, of the senses and of sensations, of those who learn by doing and experimenting. It involves the nose, touch, and the skin. And it's for those who need to try, to do, to feel. Children who touch everything and even eat stones... teenagers who have to try everything... adults who 'go by instinct'.

Why is it important to recognise their channels?

Because it helps us to tune in to our children more effectively: it's about understanding how they process information and therefore how to ensure that our messages reach their destination (beyond the woods).

Okay, that's all very well, but how will it really help me?

Finding our children's frequency helps us to:

» Build trust, strengthening the bond and magnifying the intensity of the connection;

» Reduce conflicts and related frustrations, by making sure our messages really get through;

» Improve our relationship with them, because it makes our life easier and much, much more enjoyable.

How do we do it in practice?

By carefully observing our children.

» What do they like?

» What do they avoid?

» What makes their eyes light up?

» What makes them laugh?

» What kind of language do they use?

And then? From observation, we move on to action.

Discovering their POV helps us find the most suitable frequency, or rather the channel that works best for them at a certain moment.

Once we have seen, heard and touched their favourite channel, we intentionally choose to align our communication with them.

How?

(WARNING: spoilers on the next three topics!)

...With active listening, with language, and finally with questions.

TAKEAWAYS

1. To stop your messages bouncing off your children, it helps to find out **their frequency**, i.e. their favourite channel.

2. Messages come to us and leave us through **three channels: visual, auditory and kinaesthetic.**

3. **To tune in to their frequency**, you just need to observe them and then align yourself.

10/ Beyond Words

QUESTION: Why didn't they tell me what happened? Why don't they ever tell me anything? Why do they lie?

SPOILER: After finding your children's frequency, the next step is learning how to truly listen to them.

Imagine you've just revealed a problem at work, within the department you're responsible for. You've prepared a report and are now in a meeting to discuss it with the Customer Care department. Now imagine the following scenarios.

1. As soon as you start to explain what it is about, the Management interrupts you, and plays it down, saying that it is not a real problem. 'It's trivial. A small thing'.
2. While you're talking, your interlocutor answers emails and messages. He takes a couple of phone calls, and tidies his desk. You notice immediately and suggest postponing. 'No, no. Go ahead,' he says, 'I'm busy but I'll listen to you...'
3. You explain the problem, and the Management uses sarcasm. 'You're not exaggerating as usual, are you?'
4. You've only just started talking, and here the Management stops you and instead of listening, they start with the annoying: 'Well, that's happened to me too...'
5. Before you've even finished explaining the details of the report, and above all explaining why the problem is relevant, the Management offers you a solution. 'Don't worry,' they say, 'I'll take care of it'.
6. Management immediately accuses you as soon as you start talking, claiming that if you have reached this point, you must have done something wrong.

That's not how it should be, right?

If you have detected a problem (but the same applies to an opportunity), and you have also prepared a report to illustrate it, it means that the problem exists, at least for you.

Now let's take these scenarios and move them from the company to our home.

Have we ever minimised what our children have told us as parents?

Have we ever listened to them without really listening?

Or, in good faith, have we ever tried to lighten the situation? Have we ever offered to take care of it? Have we ever said something that sounded like an accusation, again, regardless of our good intentions? 'If only you had studied'. 'I told you not to run'. 'What did you do to make your brother/sister angry?'

No parent can cast the first stone.

And this is where the difference between basic listening and Pro listening comes into play. That's active listening.

As we said a few pages ago about the frequency of our children, once we have found their favourite channel, we intentionally choose to align our communication with them, through three steps:

» Active listening;
» Our language;
» Questions.

Here we'll focus on the first step, the ability to listen to our children actively. In practice, to stay with the analogy, we'll see how to learn *to raise our antennas.*

How is it useful to us?

Active listening is extraordinarily useful in all human relationships because it connects us with the people we're talking to. It allows us to understand what they're communicating to us and helps us to empathise with them. It works at work, with friends, with people we meet for the first time and especially with the people we love.

It works wonders in our homes.

The point is that the power of listening is often underestimated and sometimes we are so busy and tired that we don't pay enough attention to the way we listen to our children.

Sometimes, while listening to our kids, we use autopilot, unwittingly slipping into the familiarity zone.

We believe we are listening to them, we sincerely think we are, and yet, we happen to be not concentrating, or to react in a way that we think is appropriate, perhaps based on a type of behavior that we have learnt and that we tend to repeat.

Do we want them to trust us, to talk to us, to open up?

Do we want to be able to guide them so they become the people we dream they will become?

Do we want to be able to help them when they are in difficulty?

Do we want them to know they can count on us?

Do we want to feel better in their company?

Less friction, more harmony?

Less shouting and sulking, more laughter?

We can always choose.

Even and especially when things get tough. Even if we think it's 'too late', like the mother in the introduction who believed she was the wrong one or the other who feared it was her child. Or that there's no way. The 'way' is there.

Intentionality is a choice: the choice to be the kind of parent we really want to be, finding our own way of raising our children, a way that is in line with who we are, with the values we truly care about, and with what we consider most important to pass on to our children.

Speaking of communication, there are two types: incoming and outgoing. As we have seen when talking about our children's channels, each child has their favourite. Once we have found it, we can learn to raise our antennas, transforming our usual way of listening to them into the 'Pro' level.

The Pro level of listening is active listening.

We call it active because it differs from the basic, routine kind, with the aim of strengthening the connection. The adjective is important because it implies, in addition to awareness, action.

How do we achieve it?

Through presence, attention, empathy.

> » When we are present, we can pay attention to our children.

> » When we are attentive, we can put ourselves in their shoes.

> » When we empathise, we can choose how to respond with more intentionality. That is, which language to use.

111

1. Presence?

By being present, I mean staying focused, on the task at hand. I put down the phone and/or laptop screen. I pause the TV series or podcast. I close the book. I turn off the vacuum cleaner, the brush, the super food processor. The Sudoku App. I stop the thousand thoughts I have in my head, the mental list of six thousand things I have to do. And I give it my full attention.

> *But what if I can't? What if I'm on a call, or at the top of a ladder changing a light bulb? What if what I'm doing can't be interrupted?*

I make sure it's something that can be postponed.
If it is, I postpone it.
'Is it OK if we talk about it as soon as I've finished [whatever I'm doing]?'

2. Attention?

Being present allows me to pay real attention, not just with my hearing, but also to see, feel, smell, what the body is saying, and to feel what the words mean.

In other (again!) words, to receive the message with all my senses.

» With my hearing to hear the words, the tone, the rhythm, the inflections, the pauses, the silences.

» With my sight, to see the expressions, the movements and the muscle contractions, the gaze, the facial expressions, the gestures, the posture.

» With my sense of smell to sniff the air, and not just in a metaphorical sense.

» With my sense of touch, in both senses, to feel the incoming message and make my presence felt without imposing it.

3. Empathy?

Presence and attention help me use empathy, allowing me to understand what the message means, what they really need, what they want to convey, and only then, how I can be useful.

Empathy is the ability to put ourselves in our children's shoes, to see their world through their eyes. And it's what allows us to choose the language we use with them and what questions to ask (we'll talk about this in the next two chapters).

When we learn to listen to our children with presence, attention and empathy, it is easier for us to recognise our familiarity zones and, therefore, to choose to take a step to the side to get out of them.

The familiarity zone of basic listening are our temptations, those that we believe are instinctive and that in fact are just habits, pure routines to which we have tamed ourselves.

Let's look at some of them and see how we can choose how to behave.

» Intervene immediately, offering to solve a problem as soon as it arises. Effect: offering advice before they ask for it could lead them to think that we don't trust their ability to solve problems. What if they don't want a solution, but just need to be listened to? Let's ask them.

» Reassure our children as soon as possible. The aim is to comfort them, of course, but if we do it too soon, we risk taking away the discomfort they are experiencing, not valuing it but stopping it in its tracks. And with it the related emotions. The problem exists, the emotions must be felt and accepted.

» Playing down, minimising or joking about it, like the Management in the initial story, regardless of our good intentions, does not give value to what they feel.

» Giving our point of view straight away. As above, our intention is good, but by doing it too quickly we could prevent our children from expressing themselves freely, from telling us how they feel, again, what they feel.

» 'The same thing happened to me'. It's wonderful to share our experiences with our children, but doing it quickly - and especially too often - shifts the attention from them to us. I know: the temptation is strong, and it is for everyone, but giving in to it stops us listening to what our children have to say.

Three practical tips to practise active listening

1.   Maintain eye contact. Look them in the eye.
2.   Bite our tongue to resist the temptation to speak before we have listened.
3.   Ask open questions about what they have just said using THEIR words (we'll talk about this in a moment).

Listening to our children in an active, intentional way is more than a way to reduce conflict, improve the atmosphere at home, and help us to help them better: while we really listen to them, we are instilling a skill that will help them for the rest of their lives.

TAKEAWAYS

1. **Active listening is the Pro level of listening** that is learnt by choosing presence, attention and empathy.

2. **Presence** helps **attention** and attention helps **empathy**.

3. When you are empathetic, **you can choose how to respond with more intention**. That is, which language to use.

11/ Words matter

QUESTION: But weren't words just words?

SPOILER: Words create worlds, choosing them intentionally helps you and your children, starting today and forever.

Words are not just words. And one is not the same as the other. The words we use are seeds that we plant in the thoughts and lives of our children, as well as in our own and those around us.

Just as when, a few pages ago, we talked about emotions, and how giving them an appropriate name helps us to experience them better, language does not just describe the world: it creates it.

> *You're not exaggerating, are you?*

Not at all.

> ## «Language was invented to serve certain specific purposes.»
> David Foster Wallace

Since the dawn of time, the first specific purpose of language has been to transmit information.

'This mushroom is poisonous. If you eat it, you will die[13].'

It will be ready soon. Come to the table.

The number you have dialled has been disconnected or is not reachable. Please try again later.

Yet the effects of language go well beyond the transmission of information.

» Language creates reality. It gives it form. It models and changes it, for better or for worse, with two effects, one immediate and one long-term. It works with us (see the *beacon* 'Our inner script') as much as with our children.

---

13   David Foster Wallace, from "Authority and American Usage" in "Consider the Lobster".

119

» Language shapes identity. What we choose to say to and for them becomes part of their inner dialogue, influencing their thoughts, their very way of communicating and the filter through which they perceive themselves and the world.

» Language is like love: a drug in the etymological sense[14], that is something that can cure, strengthen, heal, but also poison and intoxicate.

The way we talk to our children today will influence the way they talk to themselves in the future.

The language we use has immediate effects on a physical level. And it does so regardless of our awareness.

We're proud of you.
You're a wonderful wonder.
Why don't you ever do what I tell you?
Of course we're happy, but...
Don't run or you'll get dirty, sweat, etc.
Don't climb or you'll fall.
Don't talk with your mouth full.
Your room is a mess. You're always the same.
Yes, okay, you've tidied up, but...
How many times do I have to repeat it before you listen to me?

By intentionally choosing our language, we can transform not only our perception, and therefore our reality, but also that of our children.

---

14   From the greek word "pharmakon", remedy and poison.

We talked about this in relation to self-talk (*beacon* no. 7, 'Our inner script'). When we say something negative about ourselves out loud, perhaps out of modesty or because of the cultural habit of minimising our successes, we're not just expressing an opinion, we're sending a message.

And the first person to hear that message is us.

What if instead of saying 'I'm a disaster as a parent' we said 'I'm learning to become the kind of parent I want to be'? This subtle change in language changes the narrative. It shifts the focus from the problem to its solution, work in progress, 'wow in action'.

Even the way we choose to narrate events changes our perception of them, especially when it comes to unpleasant situations.

I'm talking about tone, timbre and speed.

And changing our perception, in the long run, changes our memory.

To give a practical example, I'm reminded of a client of my father's (the super coach who was born wise).

For several years, Julie had been in a lawsuit against a government agency. Despite having every right she feared that she would never win the case, also because her lawyers kept telling her to abandon it. From a purely economic point of view, it would have been better for her to give in, but it was a matter of principle for her: knowing that she was right, she absolutely did not want to give up. At the same time, she was so angry that she couldn't sleep. And in the long run, the sleep deficit was having repercussions on her whole life, including her results as a professional athlete. She felt trapped and asked my father how to get out of it.

He listened to the flood of words (swear words, mostly!) until the end, and then suggested a new approach to the story.

'Tell me the same story again, as if I were five years old and you wanted to make me laugh.'

'Once upon a time, there was an ugly, bad creature...'

My father helped her to reword the story until everything that could evoke her frustration and trigger her anger was excluded from the narration. He taught her to make a high-pitched voice, as if she were joking about a hilarious story.

'Once upon a time there was a group of poopies who worked in an office made entirely of poopies, and those little rascals...'

When she heard herself say this, Julie laughed.

It was the first time she'd been able to laugh about the case. A few weeks later, she told my father that the storytelling technique had worked great, even though she didn't believe in it at all at first.

Choosing our language is a habit we can acquire and that will help us become the kind of parents we really want to be.

At the beginning it requires a little more awareness, and it may seem strange, perhaps a little unnatural, but only because it's still new to us. The more we repeat it, the easier it will become, until we memorise it and can repeat it effortlessly.

FROM IDENTITY TO ACTIONS

'You're lazy'.
'You're a slacker'.
'You're always angry'.
'You're spoiled'.

When we use the verb "to be" we are attacking our children's identity.

Of course we want the best for them, and using the verb "to be" blames the person not the behavior. As well as being unpleasant, in the long run this can turn the message into a self-fulfilling prophecy.

'I'm just too lazy...'
'I'm just a slacker...'

When we attack a person's identity, we destroy the relationship we have with them. What we need to address is the wrong behavior.

Also beware of the 'emotional theft': when we are having a discussion and we focus on the action but the other person starts attacking your identity, we must bring the focus back to the action/topic and not fall into the trap of blame and guilt.

To explain, I'll tell you what happened when Viola was 12 years old. At the time my father had given her a phone and after a while Viola had started insisting that she too had access to social media. She was still a year away from the agreed age (remember? A few clear and firm rules) and every time she brought up the subject again, I would reply:

'Yes, I understand that you want them, I know it's important to you, and you know that we've talked about why it's better to wait: your brain is still a work in progress and needs to be ready for all the responsibilities that come with being on social media...'

Except that one evening, after my intentional response, she snapped.

'But come on', Viola said to me, very angrily, 'why can't you be like all the other mums? Why do you always have to be like this?!'

Here comes a potential *emotional theft*.

While I had remained neutral, she shifted the focus on to me, on my identity, and consequently was aiming to trigger my emotionality.

If I had reacted on autopilot, I could have felt frustrated, giving her the chance to control my emotions. In practice, stealing them from my control.

What did I do? In recognising the possible *theft*, I chose to stand my ground. In a gentle way and with unshakeable firmness.

FROM NEGATIVITY TO POSITIVITY

Let's learn to focus more on positive things, events and behavior, and less on others.

Let's learn to reward success, to praise our children, to remind them that we are there for them and that we love them always and in any case.

Won't too many compliments hurt?

I know: some parents are convinced that they can't keep telling their children that they're fantastic. These convictions are often rooted in those who grew up with a very strong sense of duty, learning to see the negative things before the positive ones.

But also in those who criticise positivity in general: 'The world is difficult. It's my job to prepare them! If I fill them with compliments they'll never get used to it...'

This type of mentality often leads to not giving any reinforcement or to offering 'constructive' criticism.

> *You only did what you are supposed to do. Why should I tell you that you did well?*

> *You already know you did well, I don't need to tell you...*

> *If I applaud all the time, I'll make you arrogant.*

What about the so-called 'constructive criticism'?

> *When I think you didn't give your best, I feel obliged to tell you.*

> *If I criticise you, it's for your own good.*

The problem is that, even if we add the adjective, criticism is still criticism. It puts our brain on alert.

When someone criticises us, we defend ourselves by justifying ourselves or attacking. And the 'construction' goes for daisies.

On the other hand, positive reinforcement is the only thing that really helps, the only thing that opens our brains and predisposes them to improvement. It works with us and even more with our children because it gets them used to believing in themselves and to doing better and better.

So?

» Let's formulate positive sentences, inviting them to do something rather than not to do something else.

» We start with 'when you...' and describe the behavior objectively.

» We continue by saying 'it happens that ...' and emphasise the effects that their behavior has on us or on others.

» We clarify how we feel at that moment.

» We conclude with 'I wish you would / I'd prefer it if you / I'd like you to' and suggest a solution that works for both of us.

FROM RANDOM TO INTENTIONAL LANGUAGE

Our aim is to help them grow, right? To help them feel good today, face challenges, etc. And to become the people we hope they will become tomorrow.

To guide our children's behavior, we can choose to use language strategically.

For example, by being mindful of *trap* words and *boomerang* words, and finally, choosing some magic words.

Traps and boomerangs

CALM DOWN

Have you ever had someone tell you to calm down when you're spinning out of control? Well, the same pleasure you feel, your kids feel too.

NOT and NO

We've already talked about this, but just to repeat and help memorization let's remember that our brain processes negations badly.

Don't think about the elephant.

Don't think about the elephant.

You're not thinking about the elephant, are you?!

'No' and 'don'ts' break the relationship and close the door on options. Instead of reacting with NO, let's say: 'Yes, I understand that you feel that way/that you want to do this...' In this way, we validate the state of mind and take the conversation where we want it to go.

TRY and SEEK

Both involve the possibility of not succeeding.

'Try focussing more at school'.

'Try finishing your homework'.

The most powerful alternative is 'DO'.

'Put the shoes away before going up to your room'.

'Do your exercises before going out'.

BUT

If we use it after a positive sentence, it nullifies it.
'You were great, but ...'
'I like the gift, but ...'
If we use it at the beginning of our answer, it says that what we want is more important. My daughter says to me: 'Mom, you know I really want pizza?' If I reply: 'But I've made gnocchi' it's like saying: 'Okay, you may want some too, but who cares'.

Alternative?

'Gee, really? I'd love some too. I made gnocchi tonight. Would you like to eat it tomorrow?'
We replace the 'BUT' with 'AND'. My son says something and instead of replying with 'yes but' (which means that I haven't listened to understand, but to reply) I say: 'Ok, let me understand correctly: you're saying that...', I use his words to make it clear that I have listened to him) and then I use 'AND', which is a subjunctive and not an adversative like 'BUT'.

Should we really abolish 'BUT'?

We can consciously use 'but' in sentences like: 'The test didn't go well, but you have great potential to improve'.

HOPE

It makes us passive, taking away our power to make things happen. Instead of 'hope', we prefer to ACT and its synonyms.

I hope the test goes well. –» I know you'll do your best in today's test.

I hope I pass. –» I'll do my best to pass.

Magic words, do we have any?

Oh yes. Here are some of the most powerful.

IMAGINE

The verb *imagine* opens up worlds.

Our brain doesn't distinguish between reality and imagination. We use 'imagine' to stimulate creativity and possibilities.

YES

Yes opens up possibilities, creates a positive atmosphere and strengthens the connection, because it makes both the person saying it and the person hearing it feel good.

And beware of 'Yes, but...'!

EASY, EASILY

Convince your brain that it's easy!

For something difficult, instead of: 'It's difficult', let's say: 'It's easier than you think'.

WHEN

When is predictive and implies certainty. Instead of 'If you finish your homework', let's say ' When you finish your homework...'

TAKEAWAYS

1. **Language creates reality, shapes identity and is like love**: choosing it intentionally helps you, starting today, and them forever.

2. **Be careful with trap words and boomerangs,** choose the magic words that help you guide your children.

3. **Choosing your language is a habit you can acquire** and that will help you become the kind of parents you really want to be.

12/ QUESTIONS

QUESTION ABOUT
QUESTIONS: the
question is how
on earth to ask
questions.

SPOILER: More
intentional questions,
more meaningful
answers

The door opens. Viola walks in, the weight of her backpack dropping to the floor with a thud, followed by the sound of one sneaker squelching, then the other.

'Ciao amore how was school?'

'Fine," she says without stopping, and as I glance up from my desk, I see her heading toward her room. I push a little further. "It was really fine?'

'Great', she answers, halfway to her room.

Great?

'Great?'

'Everything went well? Really?'

She pauses. 'Yes' and then heads back towards her room. I hear the handle. She's locked the door.

Hmm. Something doesn't add up. I have the feeling that there's more to it. Okay. I could go to her room and try again from a different angle. I don't know, maybe I could ask her if there was a problem. Maybe there was a test, or a surprise quiz. Or maybe something happened with her friends. Of course, I could be wrong. After all, she did say 'great'. Or did she? And if not, why won't she tell me? Why doesn't she want to talk to me about it?

But even if everything really went well, why doesn't she want to tell me how it went? Why doesn't she feel the urge to share her day with me?

Have you ever found yourself in the kitchen, in the car or on the sofa waiting for an answer that doesn't come, or doesn't come the way you'd like it to?

We've all been there.

You ask, but they reply with monosyllables.

You want to know everything, to hear the full story, yet all you get is a few short words:

Yes.

No.

Good.

And then, in our heads, the *why*, *where*, *when*, and *how* start:

Why don't they talk to me?

Why don't they want to tell me anything?

Why do they find it so hard to answer me?

Where did I go wrong?

When did it happen? When did they change?

And if they need a hand, how can I help them if they won't talk to me?

The story I've just told you is my own and happened a few years ago. Viola came home from school one day and replied to my question with 'fine, just fine'.

Too bad Spider man mode had already kicked in, the one with the spider sense that amplifies predictive abilities. Although I had sensed that there might be something else, on that occasion I had decided not to insist.

Intentionally, I chose to let go, not asking anything further, but instead, I went and gave her a welcome-home kiss.

A couple of minutes later, I heard the handle of her bedroom and Viola had joined me in the kitchen.

'Mum...'

'Sì amore?'

'Today at school didn't go exactly well...'

And here's the thing with questions:

» The quality of our questions determines the quality of their answers.

» The quality of our answers determines the type of parents we decide to be.

Questions are our most powerful tool.
Some spark dialogue; others shut it down.
Some open doors wide, others... less so. If words are drugs (like love), questions are one of the most effective active ingredients. All you need to do is understand their nature, the doses to administer and the relative timing.
In other words, all you need to do is read the 'instruction manual'.

OUR QUESTIONS

Let's start with 'administration', that is, how to ask our children more intentional questions, capable of opening up dialogue and strengthening our connection with them.

When asking them, let's keep an eye on three elements:

1. *Their* timing;
2. *Our* attention and the way we approach them;
3. *Our* intentionality.

Their timing

When should we 'administer' the questions?

Bombarding them as soon as we see them, when they come back from school, or get into the car, risks making them feel like they're being interrogated.

'Everything OK?'

'Yes?'

Period.

Let's leave them alone and do something else. Let's give them space to decompress, without pestering them straight away. We wait, we observe, and then we choose the right moment to ask, when they are more open to talking.

Our attention and our attitude

Let's make sure we are in active-listening mode, that we are there for them: before asking our children a question, let's make sure we can really listen to them. Make sure that our tone is curious, that it shows that we are genuinely interested, and that when we ask them a question it is out of genuine interest, certainly not to control them.

Our intentionality

Choose stimulating questions, preferring those that encourage reflection.

Avoid dead-end and inquisitorial questions.

» Dead end questions: those that pretend to be open-ended but are actually closed. Like 'How was school?'

» Inquisitorial questions: those that imply judgement and/or criticism, and instead of helping them open up, put them off. Like those that start with 'why'.

'Why did you head-butt your friend?'
'I don't know why. I just did it'.

When we ask 'why', we often unintentionally put our children in defence mode, leading them to justify themselves, and/or to explain why they did or didn't do something.

It also happens to us as adults. When someone asks us why we did something, or why we didn't achieve a certain goal (like a budget, for example), we automatically tend to list the reasons.

'Because of the market, because of the customers, because of the products...'

Instead of asking: 'Why did you hit your brother?' which usually leads to a chorus of 'He started it!' or 'I don't know!', let's say: 'I understand that you feel angry. In this family we do not tolerate violence, so find another way to express your anger'.

From 'Why are you so nervous?' we move on to: 'It seems like there's something bothering you. Do you want to talk about it?'

This approach shifts the focus from blame and justification to validating their feelings and resolving possible conflicts.

It's like transforming a confrontation into a collaboration, creating a space in which our children feel safe and are more inclined to open up and share without the anxiety of control and judgement.

THEIR QUESTIONS

Just as our questions are important, so are theirs.

When our children, from zero to seventy years old, ask us a question, they don't just want answers, they are trying to understand their world and in the meantime they are putting us to the test.

The way we respond shapes their curiosity and their trust.

In choosing our answers, we raise our antennas, entering into active listening mode:

1. Clarifying what they need. 'Do you want advice or do you just want me to listen to you?'

2. Encouraging independence. Let's guide them with 'That's a great question. What do you think?'

3. Always preferring sincerity. The tough questions come, and when they do, let's force ourselves not to lie.

Speaking of difficult questions and sincerity

Your child comes home and asks you if Santa Claus really exists. Confusion. Apoplexy. Panic.

The question itself is also simple.

'Does he exist or not?'

And yet it's a test of trust, one of the cornerstones of any human relationship, and the basis of our relationship with our children. If we dodge the question or give a misleading answer (see: fake), we risk starting to undermine it.

What now?

It happened to me a few years ago. Leonardo comes home from school and, as cute as a button, asks his question.

'Are you Santa Claus?'

Ladies and gentlemen, the Dilemma is upon us!

On the one hand, the magic: I don't want to break the magic, I want him to enjoy it a little longer...

On the other hand, the truth: '*The representation and the contextual narration of Santa Claus is a Coca Cola invention dating back to 1931 when the corporation's marketing department asked illustrator Haddon Sundblom to draw Santa Claus for its Christmas advertisements. Since then, these depictions have changed the way Santa Claus is represented: dressed in red, with a thick white beard and a contagious smile*'.

This is the real truth. It's how things actually went with Santa Claus (from Coca-Cola's official website).

Since the eyelid of the person reading this has probably just dropped, if we use it with our children we'll get the same yawning effect.

'Difficult' questions test us: when our children ask us one, like that of Santa Claus, they're not just looking for an answer about the magic of Christmas; they're checking to see if we're being honest with them.

Once again (in the name of the power of repetition!), this dilemma teaches us that, as parents, our words have an extraordinary influence.

With Leonardo, my approach was intentional. Instead of answering with a simple yes or no, I asked him: 'What do you think about it?'

'Well, Dylan told me that he's his mother,' he replied.

'And what do you think? What you think is the most important thing'.

'I think that Santa Claus lives at the North Pole, but the

part of the story where he goes to all the children in the world in one night doesn't make sense. So Dylan was right, wasn't he?'

This is a perfect moment for truth and imagination to coexist.

I confirmed his logic by saying:

'Yes, Dylan was right about that part: I'm the one who puts the presents under the tree'.

When he asked me, 'Why did you lie to me?' I answered honestly and kindly.

'I didn't lie. I wanted to share the magic with you, because believing in the things that make you happy is important'.

This kind of response respects our children's intelligence and at the same time encourages them to keep their sense of wonder alive.

We are telling the truth and at the same time showing that believing in magic and joy is something worth preserving, even when they grow up and logic begins to take over.

Ultimately, Santa's dilemma reminds us that every difficult question is an opportunity to deepen the bond with our children through honest and thoughtful communication.

Different ages and different needs

As our children grow, their needs change: when they are very young, they need above all reassurance, and then gradually they need stimulation, increasing logic and more detailed questions (and answers).

In the appendix we will look at each age group in detail. For the moment, let's look at the questions that can help us in the different stages of our children's development.

Under four years old

Until they are four years old, we can choose questions that help them manage changes and tantrums, and make decisions more easily.

For example, 'or' questions help them make choices more quickly and leave us in control of the options that suit us.

- When they are angry, we ask questions that help them name their emotions. 'Are you feeling angry because you didn't get what you wanted, or sad because it didn't go as you thought?'
- When they refuse to go to bed, we choose fun options that reduce their resistance. 'Shall I carry you like a sleeping koala or tuck you in like a burrito?'
- When they refuse to listen to us, we maintain control and promote cooperation. 'Do you want to do it or shall we do it together?'
- When they fight over a toy, we teach them to compromise. 'Should we take turns with a timer or find something else to play with?'
- When they refuse to eat something new, we encourage

curiosity instead of pressure. 'Do you want to smell it first or give it an exploratory nibble?'

- When they say 'I can't do it', we encourage perseverance. 'Do you want to try again or should I show you a trick?'

From four to six years old

From four to six years old, we can choose questions that help to manage their growing demand for independence, their friendships and their strong emotions.

- When they don't want to get dressed, we ask questions that help them to be independent, with the strategy of offering them alternatives. 'Do you want the blue T-shirt or the red one?'
- When they have problems with a friend, we encourage empathy. 'Do you think they did it on purpose or do you think they didn't realise?'
- When they are frustrated with a task or problem, we encourage problem solving. 'Do you want to solve the problem or do you want a suggestion?'
- When they make a mess and don't want to clean/tidy up, we make it more fun. 'Shall we have a race? I'll time you and see how fast you are!'
- When they are afraid to try something new, or don't feel like it, we teach them self-confidence. 'What's the worst that could happen? And what's the best that could happen?'
- When they lie about something small, we give them an easy way to self-correct. 'I believe you, because I trust you. Did you really do/happen that?'

From six to eleven

During primary school, we can choose questions that teach responsibility, problem solving and self-awareness.

- When they forget their homework, we encourage responsibility. 'What can you do to remember to do your homework tomorrow?'
- When they blame others for a problem, we shift the focus to self-awareness. 'Which part of this problem do you think was under your control?'
- When they have difficulty with a specific subject or topic, we encourage a growth mindset. 'Is it difficult because it's new?'
- When they are frustrated with their sibling, we encourage them to consider different perspectives. 'Do you think he was trying to annoy you, or maybe he wasn't thinking about it?'
- When they don't want to tidy up, we maintain control by ensuring that the task is done. 'Would you prefer to do it now, or set a timer for ten minutes?'
- When they don't know how to fix a mistake or a mess, we encourage them to find a solution. 'What is one thing you could do now to improve the situation?'

From eleven to thirteen

During middle school, we can choose questions that help them with independence, responsibility and social challenges.

- When they are nervous, angry, or down, but don't want to say why, let's help them find a starting point to talk about it. 'Did something specific happen or do you just feel blah right now?'
- When they have friendship issues, encourage self-reflection. 'If this happened to someone else, what advice would you give them?'
- When they answer 'I don't know' to everything, encourage their brain to respond. 'If I knew, what would you say?'
- When they break a rule and rebel, we encourage responsibility. 'What do you think would be a good way to fix it?'
- When they feel overwhelmed by homework, we prevent procrastination. 'Do you want to start with the hardest or the easiest thing?'
- When they feel they can't do something, we encourage perseverance. 'What's the first thing you could change to see if you get a different result?'

From fourteen to eighteen

During adolescence, we can choose questions that help them with independence and responsibility, and at the same time encourage deeper communication.

- When they don't want to talk, encourage openness by letting them choose the type of conversation. 'Do you want to vent, ask for advice, or just distract yourself?'
- When they make a bad decision but don't want to admit it, keep the focus on growth, not blame. 'Do you want to talk about what happened or how to move forward?'
- When they have a fight with a parent/sibling, we encourage conflict resolution. 'Are you trying to prove a point or solve the problem?'
- When they don't do what they said they would do, we encourage responsibility. 'Do you want me to remind you next time or do you want to find a way?'
- When they think that life is unfair, we shape their growth mindset. 'What can you do to make things different/better?'

TAKEAWAYS

1. **How can you improve the quality of your answers?** By starting with the quality of your questions: by choosing the right moment, your attitude, and your intention to favour questions that encourage reflection and open dialogue.

2. The way you choose to answer their questions says **what kind of parents you decide to be**, and strengthens trust.

3. **Your children's questions are a way of understanding the world and putting you to the test.** Let's ask questions that help them in their progress. Let's be always sincere, using words and tones in line with their age.

Appendix: Specific Ages and Moments

Do you remember where we started? With the question, 'Are our children different from us?'

Our journey together began by exploring the generational gap, before discussing Intentional Parenting—how everything begins with us, our personal identity, and the values that guide us as individuals and parents. In the sixth *beacon*, we looked at their world, and in the seventh, we returned to ourselves, reflecting on the narratives we tell. *Beacons* eight, nine, and ten showed us how to build the 'house of trust' by first discovering our children's preferred channel of communication and learning to listen actively. The eleventh *beacon* focused on words, helping us choose more consciously which to favour. The twelfth stage of our journey explored questions, allowing us to intentionally decide when and how to ask them.

Now that this first part is complete, we move into the appendix, where we'll delve into the different age groups of our children and some specific situations. For each stage or scenario, we'll explore four key points:

» Challenges Parents may Face

» What Kids are going through

» Opportunities: What We Can do for our Children and our Relationship; What We Can Do More Intentionally

» Strategies: Practical Strategies to Help Us Be the Type of Parent We Want to Be.

FROM ZERO TO FOUR YEARS OLD

Four years is 208 weeks, 1440 days and as many
nights of constant change, from the moment they
are born until they go to nursery.
An eternity!
That's true, but even if it's a broad spectrum, let's
look at the fundamental things to keep in mind
- and put into practice - to help us be the kind of
parents we really want to be.

Challenges Parents may Face

In the early days, we often find ourselves overwhelmed by exhaustion, sleep deprivation, and the relentless pressure of this new responsibility.

Our sense of self can feel as though it is being redefined at every turn. We are no longer the centre of our own universe, but rather, we are thrust into a parallel reality where the weight of the world seems to rest solely on our shoulders. We juggle a thousand commitments, our minds racing with a million thoughts—what's for dinner, when will they sleep, why won't they stop crying?

We were told that parenthood would change us, but no one truly prepares us for the overwhelming transformation it brings. The doubts and fears that accompany the new territory are endless: *Are they hungry? Will they sleep? Will they catch a virus? What if they fall? What if they don't eat enough? Are they in the right weight range? Aren't they? Why aren't they?*

These questions become our constant companions in the early years. With little sleep and endless fatigue, we find ourselves trying to make sense of it all, as our anxious minds spiral into a state of almost permanent concern. Do we want to talk about the unsolicited advices that rain down on us? Parents, relatives, even strangers, all feel entitled to offer their opinions on how we should raise our children, often with little regard for our unique circumstances.

As soon as our kids begin to talk, we are met with the first of many challenges: tantrums. These expressions of frustration, often incomprehensible to us, only add to our mounting sense of uncertainty. Are we doing the right thing? Should we react differently? And so, the flood of advice continues.

What Kids are going through

Imagine the transition from forty weeks spent in the comforting, warm cocoon of the womb, to the vast, cold, and unfamiliar world outside. It's a startling, bewildering shift. In a matter of hours, everything they once knew is gone, replaced by a sensory overload. Their need for us becomes crucial, not just emotionally, but physically too. We become their anchor in a world that feels overwhelming and frightening.

In these early weeks and months, we are their constant reference point, their source of comfort and security. We are all they know. The bond they form with us is rooted in absolute trust, and this connection is the bedrock upon which their emotional world will develop.

As our children grow in these first 1,440 days, their physical and emotional changes occur at a breathtaking pace. Their bodies grow stronger, their muscles gain control, and their coordination improves. Their cognitive development races forward as they begin to form attachments, first to us, then gradually to others in their world. Their understanding of language deepens, and motor skills are honed in those early months. But the most crucial development during this time is the formation of emotional regulation. They begin to make sense of their feelings, learning how to express them, though it often takes time and guidance from us to shape this understanding.

OPPORTUNITIES

The first four years are an unparalleled opportunity for us to shape the foundation of our relationship with our children. The bond we form with them during this time will serve as the foundation for their emotional well-being for years to come. And so, it is crucial to prioritise connection, to validate their emotions, and to foster a sense of security that they can rely on as they grow.

What We Can do for our Children and our Relationship

During this period, it is not so much about being intentional as it is about becoming intentional. This phase is less about grand plans and more about preparation—preparing ourselves for the challenges ahead while building the bond that will carry us through.

So, what can we do for our children in these early years? First and foremost, we can help them build emotional security by creating a sense of trust. They are learning that they can rely on us, and this trust is fundamental for their sense of safety and well-being.

One of the most significant ways to encourage their development is through playful interaction.

Language is the tool with which we communicate, and through playful exchanges, we help them develop their language skills while also strengthening our bond. These early years are the perfect time to build a love of communication and self-expression. When we make time for fun, spontaneous interactions, we open the door to their curiosity, enabling them to explore the world around them with greater confidence.

What We Can Build Even More Intentionally

Intentionality comes into play when we consciously encourage their curiosity and provide a safe space for exploration. The world is a fascinating place to a child, and it is our job to help them navigate it. At the same time we must also be mindful of the words we use, for they will shape their early beliefs about themselves, others, and the world. How we communicate with them, what we say, and how we say it all plays a pivotal role in their emotional development.

When it comes to emotions, the key is to recognise them early and to validate their feelings. There are no right or wrong emotions; every feeling they experience is valid. However, it is essential to teach them how to express these emotions appropriately. It's OK to feel angry, but it's not OK to bite or hit. Helping them understand the difference between feeling an emotion and acting on it is a critical part of emotional regulation.

Positive reinforcement is one way to encourage appropriate behavior, while mirroring their emotions allows them to see that their feelings are understood. These simple techniques can go a long way in helping children develop the emotional intelligence they need to thrive.

STRATEGIES: SUPPORTING GROWTH AND DEVELOPMENT

As our children begin to assert their independence, we must be proactive in helping them build autonomy while also maintaining clear boundaries.

» One useful strategy is **offering choices rather than commands**. Instead of dictating what they should do, we can empower them by giving them small choices: 'Do you want the red or blue shirt today?' or 'Do you want to walk with me, or hold my hand?' This helps reduce power struggles and encourages cooperation.

» Another effective approach is to **reframe 'no' with redirection**. Instead of outright telling them what they can't do, we offer an alternative: 'Don't jump on the sofa!' becomes 'Let's jump on the rug!' This allows us to maintain boundaries while still providing an acceptable alternative, preventing frustration for both us and them.

» Sometimes, our children will test us—pushing boundaries, seeking to understand their place in the world. This is a natural part of their development. In these moments, it is important to ignore unwanted behaviors when possible and focus on **reinforcing the positive, not correcting the negative**. For example, if they repeat a word we don't like, our reaction may inadvertently reinforce that behavior. Ignoring it and not reacting gives the message that such behavior doesn't warrant attention.

And if they start biting?

Imagine they do.

This behavior triggers a whole series of consequences, starting with the social pressure, and the teacher calling us screaming that our child bit someone. The phone call generates worry and guilt: 'The other child's mom is going to think I'm a bad mom, and who knows what the school will say...'

'Why did they do it?' we ask ourselves.

If we've already established open communication at home and talk about emotions, this shouldn't happen. But if it does, we might need to focus a little more on this, because hurting others isn't okay.

When it happens, we simply redirect the action, giving them an explanation to uncover the mystery.

'But they should know it's not allowed...'

In reality, they don't.

It's a common concern, but we must remember that children this young are still learning social norms. They don't fully understand the concept of right and wrong, and they certainly don't grasp the long-term consequences of their actions. If biting occurs, the key is to calmly explain why it's unacceptable and offer alternatives for expressing anger or frustration, such as using words or taking deep breaths. Redirecting their behavior in this way helps them learn better coping strategies.

» Building trust is fundamental to a positive relationship. We must keep our promises, show our children that we trust them, and support them when they make mistakes—because mistakes are a natural part of learning.

» It's important to offer encouragement and comfort without judgement, allowing them to explore and learn at their own pace.

» Finally, it's essential to spend quality time with our children without a set agenda. The bond we form with them is built on shared moments, whether they are planned or spontaneous. This is not always easy when life gets hectic, but it is vital for their emotional development.

Taking Care of Ourselves

Parenting can be exhausting. At times, we may feel completely drained, physically and emotionally. It's OK to admit when we need a break. In order to be the best parents we can be, we must first take care of ourselves. If there is no co-parent available, don't hesitate to ask for help from friends or family members you trust. Remember, taking time for ourselves isn't a sign of weakness—it's a necessary step in avoiding burnout.

Three Simple Tips to Support Our Children

» Establishing Routines: Young children thrive on routine. It helps them feel secure and gives them a sense of control. Whether it's a bedtime routine or a weekly ritual like 'Taco Tuesday,' routines make transitions easier and reduce tantrums.

» Involving Them in Tasks: Giving children responsibilities, even small ones, fosters independence and creativity. Let them help at the supermarket, choose items from a list, or take part in household chores. These activities not only give them a sense of accomplishment but also help develop their problem-solving skills.

» Choosing Our Battles: It's essential to recognise what truly matters. Do we need them to sleep alone at all costs? Is potty training really urgent right now? Sometimes it's OK to let go of the pressure and allow things to unfold at their own pace.

FROM FOUR TO SIX YEARS OLD

The Butterfly Just Out of Its Chrysalis

Picture a butterfly just emerging from its chrysalis. Its wings are soft and fragile, still unfolding, yet it is already fluttering, eager to explore the world. Now, imagine this butterfly navigating its new freedom with enthusiasm but also a certain clumsy exuberance. The house is its jungle gym, the ground a bit unsteady beneath its feet. It leaves trails of glitter, sets up LEGO-shaped death traps, and occasionally flings mashed potatoes around. This is the child between four and six years old.

Challenges Parents may Face

As our children embark on this phase, we are confronted with a mix of emotions. The start of nursery school can be a time of intense separation—for both the child and the parent. For the first time, they are stepping into a world outside of our immediate influence. This is often accompanied by a swirl of emotions: anxiety, excitement, and perhaps a little sadness. It's completely normal, physiological even. We are still the centre of their universe, but gradually, their world is expanding.

Friendships begin to form, and with these new bonds come the beginnings of social dynamics. As they navigate the complexities of these early relationships, we may witness the first signs of small crises. The balance between independence and attachment becomes more delicate. Their desire to assert themselves grows, but so does their need for reassurance.

At this age, they start to realise their power. They know that their emotions, whether it's joy, frustration, or anger, have an impact on us and the world around them.

When they want something, they often want it with the determination of a little velociraptor, making their desires and needs feel urgent, even overwhelming.

It is up to us, as parents, to help them understand and express these emotions. We must validate their feelings, give names to their emotions, and help them find appropriate ways to manage them, while also establishing our boundaries

Consider the issue of screen time. At this stage, children are more than capable of becoming absorbed in screens, but we must find a balance. While technology offers entertainment and learning opportunities, we are the ones who decide how much time they spend on screens. It's important to reflect on the content they engage with, ensuring that it aligns with our values as a family. This is the perfect moment to introduce them to the concept of online safety and 'netiquette' as their digital presence will only grow.

What Kids are going through

Children between four and six are developing rapidly, both physically and cognitively. Their bodies are refining their coordination and balance, as they grow stronger and more agile. Their motor skills improve every day, and the more they practise, the more they push the boundaries of what they can do. From learning to ride a bike to mastering the art of drawing a recognisable picture, their physical capabilities are astonishing.

Cognitively, their brains are working at full speed. They are beginning to ask more complex questions, to connect dots that previously seemed unrelated, and to understand the world in new and exciting ways. Their curiosity knows no bounds. One day, they may ask, 'Why is the sky blue?' and the next, 'Why do I need to go to bed?' They are testing their independence, but they still require our guidance and comfort. They need to know that we are there for them, providing a safe space as they navigate the uncertainties of the world.

Emotions, too, are a huge part of this stage. Their emotional world is in full bloom, and it can be overwhelming at times. Whether it's a tantrum over a lost toy or the exuberance of a new discovery, their feelings run deep. They can be jubilant one moment, only to dissolve into tears the next. As their emotional regulation is still developing, it's essential that we help them process and manage these emotions in a healthy way.

Opportunities

What We Can do for our Children and our Relationship

As parents, we are in a unique position to guide our children through this pivotal stage. Our role is not only to provide comfort and stability but also to foster their curiosity, confidence, and emotional intelligence. By focussing on these areas, we can help them grow into resilient, self-assured individuals who feel confident in their abilities and choices.

One of the first things we can do is help them develop a positive mindset. At this age, they are still absorbing lessons from us, whether we realise it or not. Through the language we use and the example we set, we can help them shape a growth-oriented attitude. When they face a challenge, we can teach them that it's not about being perfect but about trying, learning, and improving.

What We Can Build Even More Intentionally

A crucial part of this process is teaching emotional intelligence. Helping them name their emotions is a vital step in emotional regulation. If a child is upset, we can guide them to identify what they are feeling: 'I see you're frustrated because your tower fell down. It's OK to feel upset'. This not only validates their emotions but also provides them with the vocabulary to express themselves more clearly.

Another key aspect of this stage is helping them develop independence. While they still need us to guide them, this is the time to start giving them small responsibilities. Whether it's helping with simple chores or making decisions about what to wear, we can provide them with opportunities to make choices and feel a sense of agency.

We can also establish routines that provide a sense of security.

Clear, consistent rules create a predictable environment where children can thrive. At the same time, we should leave room for choice and flexibility. For instance, while we may insist on bedtime being at a certain hour, we can offer them the autonomy to choose which book to read before sleep.

Strategies

At this stage, there are two key strategies we can employ to support emotional regulation and build confidence in our children: the Pause and Response Technique and the Motto Technique.

The Pause and Response Technique (Emotional Regulation)

When our child is upset, it can be tempting to react immediately. But taking a moment to pause before responding is crucial. By breathing deeply and taking a step back, we can approach the situation with calm and clarity. This pause allows us to model emotional regulation for our children. After taking a breath, we can calmly acknowledge their emotions: 'I can see you're feeling upset right now. I'm here to help'.

By validating their feelings and offering comfort, we help our children process their emotions and develop the skills to regulate them in the future. This technique fosters a sense of emotional security, helping them learn that it's OK to feel upset, but it's also important to learn how to manage those feelings.

The Motto Technique (Anchoring Confidence)

Mottos are a powerful tool for building confidence. These simple, memorable phrases can serve as a guide in difficult moments. A motto such as 'The important thing is to have fun!' or 'Your secret weapon is learning!' can help them stay focused on positive values when faced with challenges.

By repeating these mottos, we reinforce key lessons and encourage resilience. Mottos become a tool for children to lean on when they encounter difficulties, helping them to stay calm, confident, and focused. Over time, these phrases can become a source of comfort and a reminder of the values we want to instil in them.

From Six to Eleven Years Old

A Journey of Change, Challenge, and Growth

The years between six and eleven are often described as a transformative period in a child's life—perhaps not as dramatic as the change from caterpillar to butterfly, but one that nonetheless marks a significant shift. One moment, they are our ducklings, innocent and trusting, and the next moment, they are like young condors, their wings still growing but already filled with the instinctive desire to soar. Yet, despite this newfound independence, they still need the comfort and safety of the nest, a place to land when the winds of change become too strong.

CHALLENGES PARENTS MAY FACE

As they move through this stage, children test limits—both their own and ours. They want independence, the freedom to make choices and decisions for themselves, while we, as parents, find ourselves faced with the challenge of teaching them the importance of boundaries and discipline. It's a delicate balance, one that requires patience and understanding.

Primary school introduces a whole new set of challenges. Homework becomes a regular part of their lives, and with it comes the first taste of pressure—from teachers, classmates, and peers. In this phase, we face the question of how best to encourage them without stifling their natural curiosity and creativity. We want to stimulate their intellectual growth, but how do we do that without overwhelming them?

At the same time, their questions are becoming increasingly complex. No longer content with simple answers, they want to know the 'whys' and 'how' of the world around them. Their inquisitive minds challenge us to think in new ways, to explain concepts that may seem simple to us but are completely new to them.

WHAT KIDS ARE GOING THROUGH

At this age, their friendships intensify. The social dynamics between children become more complicated as they form tighter bonds and begin to navigate the complexities of relationships. This can be both exciting and difficult for them as they seek to understand their place in the world and their role within a group.

168

Cognitively, they're expanding their understanding of the world. They are connecting the dots in ways they couldn't before, asking more profound questions that demonstrate an increasing ability to think critically. 'If space is infinite, where does it end?' they may ask, challenging the very fabric of reality as we understand it. They want concrete answers, and sometimes, as parents, we may not have them.

In social situations, they start to recognise and question social rules and norms. Are rules flexible? Can they be negotiated? As they test boundaries, they are also honing their negotiation skills, often surprising us by outsmarting us in the process. It's a time of great intellectual development, but also emotional turmoil. One moment they are proud of a drawing they've made, their chest puffed out with pride; the next, they've erased it, unsure of their own abilities. Self-confidence becomes a fragile thing, constantly shifting in the face of new experiences.

Justice becomes a central theme in their lives. "It's not fair!" becomes a frequent refrain, whether it's over the division of snacks or who gets more time to play. Fairness is everything, and they are developing a strong sense of what is just and what is not. As their understanding of the world broadens, so too does their desire for equality and fairness in their interactions with others.

Opportunities

What We Can do for our Children and our Relationship

Despite their growing independence and logical thinking, children between the ages of six and eleven still rely on us for guidance and support. They need us to help them make good decisions, to reason through situations, and to reflect on their experiences. This is the stage where we can begin to sow the seeds for their future development, nurturing skills that will serve them throughout their lives.

Our focus during this period should be on building their self-esteem, fostering open communication, and helping them recognise and express their emotions. At the same time, we can begin preparing them for the challenges that lie ahead, particularly the tumultuous years of puberty and adolescence.

What We Can Build Even More Intentionally

As parents, we can give our children increasing responsibility, whether through chores or decision-making tasks. This helps them develop a sense of pride in their abilities and gives them the confidence to tackle new challenges. By focussing on the effort they put into tasks, rather than just the outcome, we help them understand the importance of the process and the value of perseverance.

We also need to help them manage their friendships, teaching them to understand others' perspectives while also learning when and how to stand up for themselves. This is a time of growth in social awareness, and it's crucial that we guide them through it with empathy and understanding.

To strengthen our connection with them, we can create our own family rituals—small moments of bonding that reinforce our relationship. These rituals provide a sense of security, offering a safe space for them to return to when the world becomes overwhelming.

STRATEGIES

The 'Cut and Paste' Strategy (Making Tasks Manageable)

If our children resist tasks like homework or household chores, we can break them down into smaller, more manageable steps. Instead of saying, 'Do your homework', we might say, 'Let's start with the first five minutes'. For tidying their room, we could begin with something simple: 'Start by putting the books away'. This approach helps reduce resistance and makes tasks feel more achievable.

'Discipline in the Right Place'

It's important to set clear boundaries for ourselves as well as for our children. We need to avoid having serious discussions in their safe spaces, like their bedroom or the dining table, which should be places of comfort and connection. If a difficult conversation needs to take place, we can say, 'Let's step aside and talk about it', and move to a neutral space. This ensures that their safe spaces remain just that—safe.

FROM ELEVEN TO THIRTEEN YEARS OLD

The Middle Ground of Tweens

This is the age of transition, the middle ground between the child they were and the adolescent they are becoming. Although glimpses of their former selves can still be seen, everything is changing. Their bodies are transforming, their emotions are in a constant state of flux, and suddenly, pleasing their friends becomes the most important thing in the world. This is a time of great confusion, not just for them, but for us as well.

Challenges Parents may Face

One moment, everything is fine, and the next, we're faced with tears, anger, and slammed doors. The mood swings seem to come out of nowhere, and we are left wondering what is going on in their heads. Is it just hormones, or is it something deeper? As they start to challenge us more openly, we are forced to confront the reality that their need for independence is growing, yet they still require our guidance and support.

Social media begins to play a significant role in their lives, bringing both opportunities and challenges. The pressure to conform, the temptation to compare themselves to others, and the risk of cyberbullying all become part of their reality. As parents, we are faced with the difficult task of helping them navigate these digital waters.

What Kids are going through

The challenges they face are vast and varied. Their bodies are undergoing rapid changes, and while we may see them as beautiful creatures in the midst of transformation, they may feel as though they've sprouted a tail overnight. Body image becomes a major concern, and they may start comparing themselves to the carefully curated images they see online or to their peers.

Sleep patterns can become erratic, and their biological clock may shift into what is often referred to as *wolf mode*, with them staying up late and sleeping in later. Alongside these physical changes come emotional tsunamis, with hormonal fluctuations causing their moods to shift unexpectedly.

OPPORTUNITIES

What We Can do for our Children and our Relationship

This is a crucial time for helping them develop emotional awareness and resilience. We need to accept their emotions and help them understand and label what they are feeling. By promoting self-awareness, we can help them build the tools they need to manage their emotions and face the challenges of life with confidence.

Encouraging emotional resilience is about showing them that setbacks are a natural part of life, not failures. It's about teaching them how to bounce back, how to learn from their mistakes, and how to approach challenges with a positive attitude.

What We Can Do More Intentionally

We can help them become more self-reflective by encouraging them to think critically about the pressures they face, whether from their peers or from social media. Rather than simply telling them what is right or wrong, we can guide them to explore the reasons behind their choices. Helping them understand their own values will give them the confidence to make decisions based on what matters most to them, rather than on what others think.

We can also teach them how to question what they see online, developing their critical thinking skills so they can differentiate between what is real and what is not. With these tools, they will be better equipped to navigate the complexities of social media and peer pressure in a healthy and responsible way.

Strategies

The Technique of Emotional Labelling

Helping them label their emotions is a powerful way to build emotional awareness. Instead of telling them to 'calm down', we can say, 'I can see you're frustrated. Is it because of school or something else?' This helps them understand what they are feeling and why.

If they are angry, we might suggest, 'Anger usually means something is wrong—what happened?'

This technique encourages emotional intelligence and gives them the language to express themselves.

The 'I Trust You' Strategy for Autonomy[15]

As they navigate their increasing independence, we can support them by saying, 'I trust you to handle this situation, and I'm here if you need me'. This helps them develop a sense of responsibility while ensuring they know they can turn to us for guidance when needed.

Through these strategies, we can guide our children through this difficult transitional period, helping them develop the skills and resilience they need to navigate the complexities of adolescence and beyond.

---

15   This strategy is great for tweens and amazing for teenagers.

TEENAGERS

The Struggle, The Transformation, The Opportunity

Long faces, sullen silences, and embarrassed glances—teenagers can often seem as though they're an entirely different species. One moment, they were our eager children, brimming with questions and energy; the next, they're acting like they've been possessed by a force beyond our comprehension. An overwhelming desire to go out, combined with an absolute disinterest in anything we have to say, seems to define the teen years.

Challenges Parents may Face

Until not so long ago, we were their heroes, their constant source of comfort and guidance. The parents they could turn to for anything, their semi-divine figures always present, always protective. But suddenly, it's as if we've fallen from Olympus. We no longer seem to possess the magic we once had. They stop idolising us. They distance themselves, become defensive, and question everything we say.

You don't understand!

Leave me alone!

They speak in a language that's barely recognisable, or, worse, they don't speak at all.

They rebel.

They ignore us.

They look at us like we're the enemy.

How do we handle this? What happened to the wide-eyed child who needed our every word?

The simple truth is that our teenagers are no longer the children they once were. As much as they may still need us, they are in the process of becoming independent individuals—individuals who will challenge us, test our limits, and push us to the edge of our patience. But even though the transition can feel jarring, we must remember that we have to let them grow and experiment. It's a tough balancing act—being a parent while letting them navigate their own way through adolescence.

And let's not forget the difficult conversations we now have to have—about relationships, sex, identity, school, the future, and all the countless dangers that seem to lurk around every corner. As they change, question us, and begin to look at the world in entirely new ways, we have to guide them more than ever, even when they seem intent on resisting our help.

What Kids are going through

Adolescence is a metamorphosis, *a crucial stage of life where children shed the behaviors and physical traits of childhood, and begin to embrace those that mark adulthood. It's a time when childish dependence on parental protection gradually fades, replaced by the need to assert autonomy and take control of their own lives in a world of adults. They are caught between two worlds: no longer children, but not yet fully grown. They are adults in progress, still very much children at heart—exquisitely insecure and vulnerable[16].*

For our teenagers, the world is complex, overwhelming, and at times, frightening.

On the inside, their brains are working overtime, forging new connections at a speed that seems to defy logic[17]. Hormones are wreaking havoc on their bodies, their moods fluctuating with unpredictable regularity. The growing pains they experience aren't just physical—there's an

---

16   The adolescent brain - What our children's minds are like and how they change', by David Bueno, professor and researcher in evolutionary Biomedical Genetics at the University of Barcelona, since 2019 holder of the Neuroeducation chair UB-EDU1st.

17   The adolescent brain - What our children's minds are like and how they change', by David Bueno

emotional toll too. Their bones ache, their muscles strain, and everything seems to be changing at once.

On the outside, they are bombarded by the relentless pressure of social expectations and media influences. They want to fit in with their peers, to be accepted by their group, yet at the same time, they long to stand out, to distinguish themselves from their friends and from us. They want to grow up, to be free, to escape the constraints of childhood. And yet, amid all this turmoil, they still need us. We may be old and embarrassing to them, *cringe* in their eyes, but the truth is that they still want our presence, even if they won't admit it.

In fact, one of the most surprising findings from recent surveys[18] shows that what teenagers desire most is not greater independence or living on their own, but more time spent with their parents. Isn't that odd? In the face of all their rebellion and distancing, they still crave our company. It's a paradox we must learn to navigate with sensitivity and care.

OPPORTUNITIES

What We Can Do for Our Children and Our Relationship

So, what can we do to help our teenagers as they navigate this tumultuous stage of life?

The answer lies in looking back and looking forward.

We look back to remind ourselves that we've all been through this, and so has every generation before us. It's part

---

18   The YMCA Parent and Teen Poll "Talking With Teens: The YMCA Parent and Teen Survey Final Report"

of the human experience.

But we also look forward, recognising that what we do now is shaping not just their present, but their future. It's an investment in the future of humanity itself.

During their metamorphosis, we can help them build a strong, confident identity rooted in their own values.

This is the time to guide them in the development of decision-making skills, to show them the importance of taking responsibility for their choices, and to help them recognise their own emotions and seek support when needed.

What We Can Do More Intentionally

As parents, we can intentionally guide our teens through this transformation, remaining firm yet fair, and always respecting their autonomy. We have to show them, both in our words and by our example, what a healthy, balanced relationship looks like. This is an opportunity to teach them the importance of mutual respect, communication, and emotional intelligence.

We can encourage their independence by setting clear, consistent boundaries, while also giving them the space to make mistakes. They must learn to navigate the world on their own terms, but we are here to support them when they stumble.

Additionally, we can help them develop an open mind by engaging in difficult conversations in a non-judgmental way. We must avoid relying on labels or stereotypes. Girls don't mature earlier, and they shouldn't be expected to always have their emotions in check, just as boys aren't inherently unemotional or uninterested in reading.

As Giulia Blasi writes in her book Rivoluzione Z[19], *'Prejudice is like teeth: when you are born, you don't have them, but it doesn't take long for them to develop'.*

By modelling empathy, we can help our teenagers understand that diversity is a strength. Tolerance, acceptance, and inclusivity are values we must instil in them, for these values will not only shape their future but will contribute to creating a more compassionate, diverse world.

---

19   Giulia Blasi, "Rivoluzione Z: diventare adulti migliori con il femminismo", Italian Edition, Rizzoli, 2020.

Strategies

Delayed Reaction to Emotional Outbursts (Building Emotional Control)

When a teenager has a meltdown or loses their temper, resist the urge to react immediately. Instead, acknowledge their feelings calmly: 'I can see you're angry. Let's talk about it when you've had a chance to cool down'. This strategy helps to manage emotional conflict and allows space for emotional regulation.

The "I Trust You" Strategy for Autonomy

Instead of imposing rules, frame their autonomy with responsibility: 'I trust you to handle this situation, and I'm here if you need me'. This encourages self-responsibility, while ensuring that they know you are available when needed.

Embrace Silence

Sometimes, the best way to connect with a teenager is to simply do nothing. Be present without pressuring them. Allow them time and space to process their thoughts. This might mean sitting in silence together—no questions, no advice, just your company. Sometimes, silence speaks louder than words.

AND THEN WHAT? YOUNG ADULTS GROW UP

Do you remember when our children were young? When sticky fingers seemed to have a permanent place on everything in the house, when bedtime battles became a daily ritual, and the flood of 'whys?' seemed endless? Those were the days when 'Mum, Dad, look!' echoed through our homes, with us rushing to respond, eager to be part of every moment.

Now, those children are adults.

It's strange, isn't it? They drive cars, have their own homes, careers, perhaps even families of their own.

It's easy to assume that our role as parents has ended. After all, they are grown now, self-sufficient, and the challenges of their childhood seem to have been replaced with new ones, ones we may not feel as directly involved in.

But just because they've grown doesn't mean we're no longer needed. Our role as parents has simply shifted. It's a different stage, one that still holds immense potential for connection, love, and influence, if we approach it intentionally. Whether they are 18 or 38, the power of Intentional Parenting remains — it can still transform our relationships and, in turn, their lives. And this time, the way we influence them has changed.

183

CHALLENGES PARENTS MAY FACE

When our children become adults, it can feel like we've been left behind. One of the most disorienting feelings for parents is the sudden shift from being the primary caretaker, the central figure, to someone standing on the sidelines, watching their children navigate the world without us. It can confuse us and, at times, leave us with a sense of loss. We no longer have the day-to-day responsibility, and while we might rejoice in their independence, there's a part of us that struggles to let go.

This period of detachment can be painful, and it often brings with it a question we must answer: how do we continue being the guiding presence we once were, without overstepping? How do we transform from omnipresent parents to mentors?

Mentors?

The word *mentor* itself is a key part of this transition. It comes from Homer's Odyssey — Mentor was the trusted advisor to Telemachus, Ulysses' son.

When Ulysses left for war, he entrusted Mentor to guide his son, not with strict command or authority, but with wisdom, subtle guidance, and support. A mentor doesn't see themselves as superior to the person they are helping; instead, they offer advice, guidance, and a safe space for their mentee to find their way.

As parents, we move from being the centre of our children's lives, providing answers to every problem and direction for every decision, to being their mentors. It's no longer our place to constantly be involved, to give unsolicited advice or to take control of their choices. They need to know that we love them, support them, and respect their ability to make decisions for themselves. Their world is theirs to navigate now, and our job is to see it from their perspective, without interfering unless they ask.

Yet, there lies a temptation to intervene. Especially when we perceive them to be struggling, or when we don't agree with the path they're taking.

It's an ongoing internal struggle — knowing when to step back and when to step in.

WHAT *KIDS* ARE GOING THROUGH

This is the time when they are becoming — or have already become — fully independent. They make their own choices now, about their personal lives, their relationships, their careers, and their identities. In many ways, they no longer need us in the way they once did, but they still do need us — just not in the same capacity.

Imagine you are driving a car while one of your parents has their hands on the wheel. Or think about when someone in the passenger seat keeps telling you how to drive...

'Why did you turn right?'

'Slow down!'

'You're going too fast!'

'Watch out!'

It's easy to fall into the trap of offering guidance, even when it's not wanted.

This is the delicate balance we must strike — they still need us, but not in the way they did when they were younger.

We must learn to respect their space to drive their own life. It's a role reversal — they're now at the helm, and we must trust them to steer, even if the road ahead is unfamiliar or filled with obstacles.

Opportunities

What We Can do for our Children and our Relationship

Even though they are now adults, this doesn't mean we stop being parents. In fact, this is the opportunity for a new kind of parenting — one that is based on mutual respect, understanding, and a shared recognition of independence.

Our goal is to continue nurturing a relationship that can last forever, one that is built on trust.

We must foster their confidence in their ability to make good decisions while also reassuring them that, should they need us, we will always be there.

Our homes are still open to them, not just physically, but emotionally.

We are here for them, ready to offer a safe space for them to return to — no matter what choices they make.

This is where the power of Intentional Parenting comes into play.

We can continue to influence their lives in profound ways, but it must be done with a light touch. The days of giving unsolicited advice are behind us. Instead, we celebrate their independence, acknowledge their growth, and remain emotionally available when they ask for guidance.

What We Can Do More Intentionally

The choice to be intentional in how we parent our adult children lies with us. We can celebrate their independence and the progress they make, while still being present in their lives. We must be available to offer guidance when asked — but only when asked. We must also recognise when we can step back and allow them to make their own decisions.

Of course, they will make mistakes. That's part of growing up. But it's essential that we allow them to choose their own path, even if that path is different from what we had envisioned for them. When they face important decisions, we can be there to ask the right questions — ones that help them think through their options, rather than giving them the answers outright. Encouraging them to trust their own judgement is one of the most empowering things we can do.

But what if they don't ask for our help? This is a question I often hear from parents who feel torn between wanting to assist and not wanting to overstep. The answer is simple, though — even as adults, our children continue to absorb our behavior, our attitudes, and our actions. They are watching us and learning from the way we handle situations. This is where the shift becomes apparent. We must model the behavior we want to see in them: patience, understanding, respect, and trust.

STRATEGIES

Declare Our Metamorphosis

We must openly acknowledge the change in our relationship. When discussing their choices, we can say, 'I'm still your mother/father, but I respect the fact that this is your life. I'm always here for you, no matter what'.

Ask for Permission Before Giving Advice

To stay connected and available without imposing ourselves, we can ask, 'Would you like my point of view on this subject?' or 'I share something that might help?' This way, we maintain our bond while allowing them to have control over the conversation.

Be Emotionally Available

We remain available to them, not just physically, but emotionally. They may come to us when they need guidance, and when they do, we must be ready to listen and offer support without judgment.

Trust Their Journey

Above all, we must trust in their ability to navigate the world, knowing that they are still learning, growing, and evolving. As parents, we must learn to step back and watch them create their own path, offering our support in a way that respects their independence.

OUR FAMILIES

The so-called 'traditional' families are a thing of the past. Today, there are simply ours. And ours are open, evolving, and varied. Yes, they are different — because each person is different.

Every parent is unique. This remains true for everyone, always: whether we raise children as biological parents, step-parents, single parents, remarried parents or adoptive parents. It makes no difference.

Every family is unique: we are never simply the parents of one, two, or one plus three children. We are part of a wider mosaic of individual stories, relationships, and dynamics which, woven together, shape who we are.

The purpose, for each of us, is to guide our children through life with care and intention.

In the pages ahead, just as we have done for different ages, we will explore some particularly challenging situations

— moments that test both us and our children. Blended families, parents who live apart, adoptive parents: specific circumstances that, by their very nature, call for greater thoughtfulness in our actions and decisions.

BLENDED FAMILIES

Step-parents –
Carving Out a Unique
and Beautiful Space
Within a Blended
Family

CHALLENGES PARENTS MAY FACE

» Case A: I meet someone, fall in love, and begin to get to know their children. We start to build a new family — part them, part me. The biological parents are there, but then there's me, the newcomer. No matter how long the relationship has lasted, I am still the *latest arrival*.

» Case B: I meet someone, fall in love, and introduce them to my children, creating a new family dynamic. While I'm still a biological parent, my partner will now raise my children alongside me. It's a shift in how we navigate our parenting.

» Case C: I meet someone, fall in love, introduce them to my children, and also meet theirs. Together, we forge a fresh family dynamic, blending two worlds into one, full of new beginnings and plenty of complex layers.

In Case A, I am the step-parent stepping into the lives of one or more children. And adapting is anything but simple. As the *newbie*, I enter into a well-established rhythm and dynamic, where everyone knows their place. The biological parent tries to support me, but they're often torn between their loyalty to their children and their desire to welcome me into the fold. It's a tricky balance to strike.

In Case B, I'm the biological parent, trying to manage the delicate dance of blending lives. I feel the responsibility to make everyone happy. I want my partner to feel included and valued, yet I don't want to force their presence on anyone. I want peace, but peace is often elusive. My children, understandably, may feel displaced. Suddenly, they are no longer the centre of my world, and jealousy or frustration might arise. Worse still, the presence of a new partner confirms for them what they've been fearing: the old family unit is truly over.

In Case C, complexity intensifies. Now, I'm not only adjusting to a new partner but also trying to navigate two entirely different family structures. My parenting style may be very different from my partner's, and my children may be wary, not just of my partner but of their children too. Trust is something that takes time to build, and it's not always smooth sailing.

In all three cases, the challenges remain strikingly similar: rejection, mistrust, blurred boundaries, and a lack of clarity regarding roles. The step-parent may feel like an outsider. The biological parent may feel caught in the middle, constantly trying to balance loyalty to both their partner and their children.

What Kids are going through

The unknown is unsettling for all of us, but for children, it can be downright frightening. A new family dynamic — particularly when it involves the introduction of a new adult — can feel like a threat. The unfamiliar often triggers feelings of insecurity and fear, and it's natural for children to resist change. After all, no matter how well-intentioned, this *new person* may feel like an imposter — someone perceived as a replacement, rather than an addition.

Children often won't embrace these changes with

open arms. While there are exceptions, they are few. More typically, what follows is distrust, frustration, disappointment, jealousy, resentment, and even anger.

Some classic phrases might be:

We don't need another mum/dad.

They're not my mum/dad — they can't tell me what to do.

I don't like them.

So you're really never getting back together?

The reality that a parent has moved on can lead to feelings of jealousy and the construction of emotional walls. Children may wonder, *Who is this person stealing my time and attention?*

OPPORTUNITIES

When a family expands, ensuring everyone feels secure and valued requires immense patience, care, and grace. But this process doesn't happen overnight — it's a journey that requires each step to be taken with mindfulness and love.

What We Can do for our Children and our Relationship

The key lies in stepping gently into the new dynamic. We must learn to recognise and validate our children's feelings without taking them as personal attacks. They're adjusting to a new reality, and their emotional reactions, while difficult, are perfectly normal.

Patience is perhaps the most underappreciated strength in our fast-paced world. Yet, when it comes to building a blended family, patience is the key that unlocks relationships. The word itself derives from the Greek *pascho* (to feel) and the Latin *patior* (to endure), reminding us that patience is rooted in passion, empathy, and perseverance. We may want immediate results, but in reality, it's the slow and steady growth that lays the foundation for something lasting.

What We Can Do More Intentionally

Creating a happy home environment, where everyone feels welcome, takes deliberate effort. It requires consistency, clarity, and clearly defined roles. Each family member — biological and step-parents alike — must contribute steadily and respectfully, through both actions and words.

As biological parents, we must remind ourselves that our children are not automatically obligated to accept this change. After all, this was our choice, not theirs. The key is to offer them love freely and without expectation. They may need time to process what's happening, and that's okay.

Defining roles is crucial. As biological parents, we can support our partners by helping them find their place within the family structure. This involves ongoing communication and ensuring there is no ambiguity or tension around roles.

As step-parents, we must resist the urge to replace anyone. We aren't substitutes. Our role is to build unique, trusting relationships with each child. It's not about taking over the parenting; it's about contributing to a healthy, stable family dynamic that works for everyone.

STRATEGIES FOR BLENDING FAMILIES

Be patient and present

We mustn't rush the process. Instead, we stay consistently available, offering gentle love and understanding. Over time, we will build trust and connection.

Keep communication open

Honesty and regular conversations are essential. Both with our partners and with our children. By listening to their doubts and worries, we can navigate through difficulties and prevent misunderstandings from becoming bigger issues.

Embrace difficulties with empathy

Adjustment takes time, and friction is inevitable. When it arises, we meet it with kindness, understanding, and thoughtfulness. Building a blended family is a long-term journey, but one day, with patience and care, we will create a unique and beautiful home where every person has their cherished place.

CO-PARENTS

Building a United Front for Our Children

'The boat of love has broken', as the poet Majakovskij said — though some days it might feel less like a boat and more like a punctured dinghy sinking in stormy waters. The romance has ended, the paths have split, and suddenly the person you once held hands with now feels like a stranger, or worse, the adversary in a courtroom drama you never auditioned for.

But between you and that person stand your children — innocent, wide-eyed observers of the entire messy situation. And it's painfully easy, often without even noticing, to pull them into the crossfire. A sigh, an eye-roll, a sharp comment muttered under your breath — children catch it all, like tiny detectives with highly sensitive antennas.

CHALLENGES PARENTS MAY FACE

Separation isn't simply a closed door; it's more like someone has taken the whole house apart, brick by brick, and handed you the blueprints to rebuild — in a storm — with one hand. The emotional earthquake is all-consuming: routines shattered, patience worn thin, and enough paperwork to bury a small village. And in the middle of that chaos, small faces look up at you, needing stability, when you barely know where your own footing is.

And on the other side, sometimes feeling miles away both physically and emotionally, is the other parent — perhaps trying to navigate the same storm, or perhaps adding to the turbulence. Conversations that should be about 'what's best for the children' quickly descend into point-scoring. A simple 'Who's picking up from school?' becomes a duel worthy of a medieval court. And in the process, we often forget to check in with the very people most affected by all this: our children.

It's perfectly natural, too, to question ourselves. *Am I doing enough? Am I messing this up? Should I have tried harder? Should I have left sooner?* The internal monologue can be exhausting. But remember — doubt means you care. It means you're trying. And that's already a strong start.

WHAT KIDS ARE GOING THROUGH

Children don't see legal documents or custody schedules; they see their world cracked open. Suddenly, Christmas is split in two, bedtime stories are read by one voice instead of two, and family traditions become memories tinged with confusion.

They might not understand why love can end. In their eyes, love is supposed to be forever, like fairy tales promised. They might cling to hope, wishing for reconciliation, or blaming themselves for the fracture. Was it something they did? Something they said?

They can feel torn in two — like they must be loyal to both parents but fear they might betray one by loving the other.

They might put on a brave face, telling you everything's fine, but inside, their emotional world is tangled.

And sometimes, just sometimes, they might attempt to manipulate the situation (children are wonderfully clever like that), playing one parent off the other for that extra scoop of ice cream or a later bedtime. Don't fall for it — but do recognise it for what it is: a sign they're struggling to make sense of shifting sands.

They are alone, they are suffering, they are afraid.

They are lost: they have suddenly lost their bearings and their old world has broken down.

OPPORTUNITIES

The first step is to remember that we always have a choice: we can choose how to react, and therefore also choose not to give in to anger or frustration.

This is the first thought, and the very first step away from the situation (we've talked about it, haven't we?) that can help us in the most difficult moments, when patience falters and even Job would give up.

But we won't, because unlike the aforementioned, we have decided that we want to be parents.

What We Can do for our Children and our Relationship

Our goal as parents must always be in front of our eyes, like a post-it note that follows us everywhere and on which there is only one question: what kind of parents do we want to be?

When we put our answer at the centre of our daily actions, every choice we make will have an impact on our children, helping them to suffer less and gradually to understand that stories can end, but not necessarily in a bad way.

Not only that.

With time, patience and open communication, we can show our children that even something as radical as a separation can be a positive choice: instead of staying in a painful relationship, for us and inevitably for them too, we have chosen to end it because we believe in love, true love.

What We Can Do More Intentionally

For them and for us, regulating our emotions is now key: recognising the different nuances, giving them an appropriate name, and learning to manage them, deciding not to let them overwhelm us. Working on our emotional responses is good for us and gives our children a positive model that is very useful for dealing with difficulties.

How they experience this phase depends on us and for this reason it is very important to create a new alliance with the other parent. Our children must see us united, aligned, cohesive and working together, both focussed on their well-being.

Our ability to remain aligned, despite the difficulties, will have a positive impact on their future. For this reason, let's remember that important decisions must be made together, not alone.

Showing respect and understanding means giving them the tools to build healthy and lasting relationships in the future.

And speaking of respect, it's not enough not to speak ill of the other parent, we must make an effort to speak well of them. Showing respect in all interactions, even when we are hurt or angry, is one of the most powerful lessons we can offer them.

And if the other parent is against it?

Let's discuss it, reminding them that we have a common goal: the well-being of our children.

Children are like sponges, and every word, every reaction and every choice leaves a permanent mark on their lives.

STRATEGIES

In love we trust

Let's rely on the therapeutic power of love. Let's show our children that, despite the difficulties, we love them unconditionally and will continue to do so. Let's talk to them, listening to them without judging them, to help them understand that, even if the separation is painful, the love of their parents never ends.

Open communication

We encourage our children to share their fears and feelings. We need to be honest and direct with them, without scaring them. We shouldn't burden them with our problems, but we can share our emotions so that they understand that we too are experiencing a change and we are there to face it together.

Routine and stability

Maintain consistent daily routines that offer security, such as regular mealtimes and sleeping times. Even in difficult times, the predictability of activities helps children feel protected and less overwhelmed by change.

ADOPTIVE PARENTS

Honouring their story and building bonds that last

Choosing to adopt is one of the most extraordinary, courageous decisions anyone can make — and, without question, one of the most challenging. The difficulty begins from the moment that decision takes root. Adoption is rarely quick or simple, neither for the parents who embark on this journey, nor for the child they welcome into their lives.

It's perhaps the only form of parenthood that begins with hurdles: forms, assessments, endless paperwork, long stretches of waiting. And yet, like every kind of parenting, it arrives without any guarantees. The ripples of every word, every action, reach far into the child's life.

Raising an adopted child is a vast and intricate subject — far too immense to be covered within the pages of one book. I won't pretend otherwise. But there are guiding principles that can help us nurture a deep, secure connection that stands the test of time.

CHALLENGES PARENTS MAY FACE

When we adopt, we step into a role that comes with challenges from every angle.

We long to pour love into our child — unconditional, unwavering, wholehearted love. But we also know they bring with them a story that's uniquely theirs, a history that has shaped how they see the world. Their story is already written in part, and we must learn to honour it. We wonder if we are enough. If we can build trust, form that all-important bond, and truly be loved in return.

How do we answer the inevitable, difficult questions?

How do we help them understand that blood is only part of the picture?

How do we become the parents they need, not just the ones we imagine ourselves to be?

What if they struggle to understand us — or worse, reject us altogether?

What if their past feels so vast, so heavy, that it sits between us like an unspoken wall?

No parent arrives in this world fully equipped for the hardest job imaginable — but adoptive parents need an extra measure of courage and resilience.

WHAT KIDS ARE GOING THROUGH

Every adopted child carries a story, one that's rarely simple. Even if they are young, or have had little contact with their birth family, their early experiences have already taught them how to view the world.

They may feel conflicted: part of them may be eager to embrace their new life, but another part might resist, unsure of how to trust again.

Some children, particularly those who've been through foster care, may keep us at arm's length, protecting themselves with defiance or silence.

They may question their origins, wonder why they are here with us, and grapple with feelings of rejection or abandonment.

They might fear they were unwanted, or that love — real love — will always be fleeting.

Their past shapes their brain and their instincts.

If they've missed out on safe, secure attachments early on, they may struggle to express emotions or regulate their behavior. Defensive or self-sabotaging actions may surface — a way of pushing us away before they fear we might leave them.

We must remember: it's not personal. It's survival.

OPPORTUNITIES

Being an adoptive parent is about far more than providing a roof over their heads and meals on the table. It's about crafting a space where connection and trust can slowly take root and bloom. It's about showing them what real, unconditional love looks like — not just in words, but in action, every single day.

This is our chance to show them that, while life may not have started as it should have, a new chapter can be written — one where love, stability and belonging are at the centre.

What We Can do for our Children and our Relationship

So, what can we do to help them and build that lasting bond?

The key lies in respecting their world-view. As we spoke about in *beacon* no. 6, we must learn to see the world through their eyes, honouring their past while gently showing them that the future holds something brighter.

When questions about origins arise, honesty is paramount, as we explored in *beacon* no. 12. We answer with care and sensitivity, always keeping their emotional well-being front and centre.

We love them without conditions. We accept them exactly as they are — every scar, every question, every ounce of baggage they carry. We strive to understand their feelings, even when they don't know how to voice them.

What We Can Do More Intentionally

Adoptive parenthood calls for extraordinary patience, empathy and fierce, unshakable love.

Every child's story is theirs alone. Our role is to honour it, gently weave it into the fabric of our family, and help them feel truly at home. We build bonds strong enough to endure storms and time alike.

This means working on ourselves — becoming a steady presence, communicating with consistency and honesty, and filling our home with warmth and joy.

We lean on rapport-building techniques: listening without judgement, validating their emotions, and creating moments of harmony.

We become their safe place — the rock that assures them they will never face rejection or abandonment again. We are not here for now; we are here for life.

We give them space and time to open up, never rushing or forcing. Their story unfolds at their pace, not ours.

STRATEGIES

We build trust, day by day

Through presence, consistency, and actions that align with our words. We show up, and we keep showing up, until they know — deep down — that we always will.

We tune in

We listen with empathy, without trying to fix or hurry them along. We accept them for all that they are, and all that they might become. No judgement. Just love.

Patience (and then a bit more patience)

We honour their timing, letting them decide when and how to face their past. When they're ready, we answer honestly, gently, and with kindness, reminding them they are safe, they are loved, and they are home.

THE END

WARMEST WISHES AND HEARTFELT HUGS

Take a moment to look back on the road you've travelled — a journey where parenting is no longer a series of reactions, but a conscious, thoughtful choice.

Picture your home as a place where trust, understanding and intentional communication are not distant ideals, or things experts talk about, but the very foundation of everyday life—some days more successfully than others, of course.

You've taken the time to explore who you are as a parent, discovered the incredible power of your words, and embraced how trust and active listening can deepen the bond between you and your children.

Along the way, you've witnessed how small, deliberate choices foster greater understanding, nurture mutual respect, and help create a home where everyone feels truly seen, heard and valued. Now, as you move forward, you'll continue shaping your family with intention — building relationships where your children feel safe, appreciated and free to grow into whoever they are meant to be.

Intentional Parenting isn't a one-off decision; it's a way of being — one that involves patience, kindness, and a good sense of humour. And now, you hold the tools to continue this journey with purpose, knowing that the parent you choose to be today will help shape the world your children will build tomorrow.

ABOUT THE AUTHOR

My name is Giulia, and I am the proud mother of Viola and Leonardo. My purpose is to help change the world — starting with my own children. To do that, I have made a conscious choice: to choose what kind of parent I wish to be, every single day.

My name is Giulia, and my mission as an Intentional Parenting Coach is to help other parents understand that there is no single way to be a parent. And that the key is to take your role as a parent seriously, without taking yourself too seriously...

I run workshops and conferences, both in person and online, offering group sessions and one-to-one coaching tailored to individual needs. I also write regularly, sharing thoughts and guidance on my blog: giuliagalli.substack. com.

Share this book, what you have taken away from it, what you liked about it with other parents, friends and family. Leave it in a nursery, gift it to someone in need of inspiration, or hand it casually to another parent at the playground. What matters most is that it continues its journey, sparking meaningful conversations and helping to grow our community.

ACKNOWLEDGMENTS

To my mum and dad, Michela and Bruno, who raised me to be strong and independent, always encouraging me to be wholly myself and loving me unconditionally for it.

To my husband, Giacomo, who has grown with me over the years, standing beside me through life's twists and turns, and who embraces, with care and joy, the wonderful adventure of raising our marvellous children together.

To my sisters — Chiara, Anna and Maria — my companions on this lifelong journey. They are by my side through the laughter, the tears, and all the moments in between. I truly couldn't wish for a better sisterhood.

To the parents who generously shared their stories — to those who appear in these pages under a pseudonym, though their experiences remain entirely real. To the parents who have spent countless hours asking themselves questions, seeking to do better; and to those who are only just beginning on this path.

And lastly, to my dear friend Roberta Giulia Amidani — writer, thinker, and futurist — whose guidance and insight helped me shape this book with you in mind: you, the reader who holds it now in your hands.

Giulia Galli
When a Parent is Born
Your Journey Toward Intentionality

All Rights Reserved
Copyright © 2025
1st Edition April 2025

Reegal
DEEPENING ROOTS

REEGAL.CO.UK
GIULIAGALLI@SUBSTACK.COM

Printed in Great Britain
by Amazon